THE
NEW
AMERICAN
CUISINE

Acknowledgments

Many friends and colleagues have contributed their time and talents to this volume. In particular, I must thank Derek Hastings for his valuable suggestions and favorite recipes. My editor, Sheila Rosenzweig, was enthusiastic and helpful as always. And lastly, my thanks to Tony Meisel, whose idea this book was.

THE
NEW
AMERICAN
CUISINE

Edited by Judi Olstein

GALLERY BOOKS
An imprint of
W.H. Smith Publishers Inc.
112 Madison Avenue
New York, New York 10016

For Mom and Dad

Published in the United States by
Gallery Books
An Imprint of W.H. Smith Publishers, Inc.
112 Madison Avenue
New York, NY 10016

This book was designed and produced by
Footnote Productions Ltd.
6 Blundell Street
London N7 9BH

Composition by *Paragraphics*
Color origination by Hong Kong Scanner Craft, Ltd.
Printed by Lee Fung Asco Printers, Ltd.

Editorial Director: Sheila Rosenzweig
Art Director: Liz Trovato

Contents

Introduction

Recently all the talk in culinary circles has been, and continues to be, about the "new" cuisine. The new Italian cuisine, the new American cuisine, *nouvelle cuisine*...whatever nationality or region, there is a new and revolutionary version of it...or so we are told. Like much that is bandied about as radically different, the new cuisine is really an exploration and extension of existing culinary traditions.

A hundred years ago, Escoffier said *"faites simple"*...make it simple. Unfortunately, few have ever followed this advice. The net result, of course, has been to make every excursion through the kitchen an excuse for the loud trumpeting of revolution. Yet what is happening today is not much different from what took place between the wars, when Fernand Point undertook his clarification of the classic French cuisine. With audacity and wisdom, he was able to take the fossilized (at least by that time) work of Careme, Escoffier, Durand and others and build on it, gradually bring it back to its roots, search out purer and more intense flavors. In the process, he trained many of the chefs who were the grand old masters before the current rage.

Perhaps the efforts at publicity of the current trumpeting angels of the new cuisine have been too successful. How else to explain the excesses committed in their names, the travesties on good taste? Food is only truly successful if it is above all honest, and honesty demands craftsmanship, fine ingredients, expert timing and a sense of proportion. This last is perhaps most important. No amount of kiwi slices or puff pastry cases will make what goes under or in them taste good. After all, is not the flavor of food the most important aspect of good cooking?

This sense of proportion, coupled with renewed interest in a diet more appropriate for the way we now live, is responsible for almost all of the new cuisine. Whether it is Alice Waters at Chez Panisse in California or Pierre Koffman at Tânte Claire in London or Georges Blanc at La Mère Blanc in France, they all are searching for the honest flavors of the natural ingredients they cook with such simplicity and panache. No cauldrons of pig's feet or mounds of starch for these masters. Rather, light, elegant cooking, food that is healthful and still tastes wonderful.

The key to the new cuisines it to search out the best ingredients, combine them with restraint, cook them with precision and present them with artfulness—not much different from the best cooking of any generation.

One of the most interesting aspects of the new cuisine is its imaginative use of new ingredients and its combining of ingredients not usually thought of as complementary. Oriental cookery has had its impact here, much as Oriental art was so informative for the Impressionist painters of the late nineteenth century. Herbs, roots, berries and fungi virtually unknown have been brought into the currency of Western cooking. And their textures and tastes have had a startling impact in transforming the pedestrian, everyday raw materials we are so familiar with into ravishing and exotic dishes.

Likewise, creating new tastes by counterpointing flavors previously thought unsuitable according to the classic canons has led to some wild combinations, but there are often historical precedents for them. The use of fruit with meat or fish is a good example, yet Northern European and Polynesian cookery abounds in traditional combinations of this nature. Such combinations, in fact, are perhaps more foreign to a Frenchman than to an American Southerner or a Northern Italian. Witness the Southern American use of peaches with ham, or the Northern Italian *agrodolce* sauces for game, which combine chocolate, sultanas, nuts and spices. Much of the new cuisine, to stretch the point just a bit, harks back to some of the combinations of late medieval cookery, with its contrasts of sweet and sour, hot and cold, crisp and soft.

Contrast is important. No one wants to eat a plate of white fish accompanied by mashed potatoes and cauliflower. The purity of it is just too much for the stomach to contemplate. Besides contrasts of taste, contrasts in appearance are vital to the new cuisine. Artistry at the stove can be negated if the same artistry is not present on the plate. Once again, the Oriental influence is evident, especially the Japanese. Part of the appeal of the new cuisine is its painterly quality. Presented with a plate literally "pretty as a picture," one is almost hesitant to disrupt the integrated art of it all. Yet all the cook is doing is enticing the diner, reinforcing the sense of anticipation of what he or she is about to taste.

The new cuisine is also part and parcel of the current concern for healthier foods, fewer fats and starches and shorter cooking times. Not only is this trend leading to better eating in a medical sense, but also to a greater appreciation of the true tastes of food, unblemished by heavy sauces and charred surfaces. A fish simply grilled over mesquite wood or vine cuttings and served with nothing more than a squeeze of lemon or lime savors of the sea and freshness. Doused with cream and wine the same fish may taste wonderful, but it does no good to the arteries or heart or waistline, and what one tastes is the cream and wine, not the fish.

What the advocates of the new cuisine are trying to do is not upset traditions and preferences but refine them. In doing so, they have added a new excitement and sensibility to the table. Cookery is always evolving. We are lucky to be living in an age where the resources and imagination for such an evolution are so abundant. *Bon appetit!*

A Note About Measurements

The recipes for this book were created for international use. To that end, measurements are given in approximate American, Imperial and metric equivalents. It is important to remember that the American and Imperial systems are equivalent for solid weights; they differ only for liquid measures. In addition, 1 Imperial tablespoon equals 1¼ American tablespoons. However, this book was written to be easily used, and not as a test of measuring skills. In virtually no case will a minor variation in measurement affect a recipe in any significant way.

Temperatures throughout this volume are given in Fahrenheit and Celsius. An equivalency chart for cookers using the gas mark system is given below.

Fahrenheit	Gas mark
225	¼
250	½
275	1
300	2
325	3
350	4
375	5
400	6
425	7
450	8
475	9

Beginnings

The start of any meal is much like the raising of the curtain at a theater. You take in the scenery, the lighting, the props and the actors in costume. That first impression must hold the audience for the action to come. Equally, the first food on the table must whet the appetite for more. And it must interact with the cutlery, glassware and china, the linens and accoutrements to create an ambience of well-being and comfort. Curtain up! Only this time for a meal.

If what starts any meal sets the tone for what follows, it must be remembered that what follows cannot be ignored. The opening salvo cannot be allowed to overwhelm what follows, either in substance or in complexity. The days of formal dinners with several hors d'oeuvres and two soups are far, some might say thankfully, gone. A slice of pâté, a cup of clear soup, a few refreshing and crunchy tidbits will suffice to pique appetites, if the food is irreproachably fresh and served with artistry and panache.

One rule to follow is never start a meal with a dish that evidences any sort of sweetness. Sweet foods suppress the appetite, and unless you are planning to serve a main course of such meagerness as to drive your guests and family away, you should remember this simple dictum. Forsake fruit salads and confections of any kind. Make the appetizer or soup light enough to keep the assembled company wanting more. Keep in mind the seasonal produce when you plan your menu. This is especially true of openers. Don't burden diners with a steaming bean soup in the middle of summer or an icy aspic in winter. If a particular vegetable is fresh and abundant, devise a simple dish to present it at the height of flavor.

Most importantly, begin a meal with something that suggests a sense of occasion. It need not be caviar or a lavish mousse. An artfully arranged salad or a steaming bowl of consommé, presented with flair and care, can make the meal to follow as special as a night at the theater. The first course can set the stage for the applause at the end of the evening.

Baked Whole Garlic

8 large whole garlic heads
2 cups (450 grams) sweet butter
2 sprigs fresh rosemary or 1 teaspoon dried
2 sprigs fresh oregano or 1 teaspoon dried

Preheat the oven to 375°F (190°C).

Remove the papery outer layers from the garlic heads, leaving the cloves and heads intact.

Place the whole heads on a large sheet of thick aluminum foil. Top each head with equal amounts of the butter and herbs. Fold up the foil around the heads and fold it sealed.

Place the packet of garlic on a baking sheet and bake for 1 hour, or until the heads are soft.

Remove the packet from the oven and open the foil. When just cool enough to handle, squeeze the baked garlic cloves from the skin. Spread the cooked cloves onto thinly sliced pieces of crusty bread or pumpernickel and serve hot.

serves 8

Bacon and Tomato Rounds

½ pound (225 grams) coarsely chopped
  bacon
4 tablespoons (60 grams) sweet butter,
  softened
1 tablespoon drained prepared white
  horseradish
salt to taste, if desired
freshly ground black pepper to taste
28 very thin slices whole wheat bread
7 cherry tomatoes, stemmed and halved
  lengthwise

Cook the bacon in a skillet over moderate heat until it is golden brown and crisp. Remove from the skillet with a slotted spoon and drain on paper towels. Allow the bacon to cool completely.

Place half the cooled bacon, the butter and the horseradish into the container of a food processor or blender and process un-

til smooth. Place the mixture into a bowl and season to taste with salt and pepper. Cover the bowl and let stand in a cool place for 2 to 2½ hours.

Trim 14 slices of the bread into a circular shape with a diameter of roughly 2¼ inches (6 cm). Spread 14 of the rounds with the bacon mixture and sprinkle them with the remaining bacon.

Cut circles with a diameter of roughly 1¼ inches (4 cm) from the centers of the remaining bread slices to make rings. Reserve the centers for another use and top the 14 buttered rounds with the bread rings. Place a tomato half, cut-side down, into the center of each ring and serve.

serves 4

Stuffed New Potatoes

24 very small new potatoes, unpeeled
boiling water
1 cup (225 grams) sour cream
¾ cup (180 grams) black or golden caviar

Wash and dry the potatoes. Place the potatoes into a large saucepan with enough boiling water to cover. Quickly bring the water back to a boil, then reduce the heat and cook until the potatoes are tender but still firm, about 10 minutes.

Drain the potatoes and immediately drop them into a bowl of cold water. When potatoes are cool, drain again and pat dry. Cut a thin slice from the bottom of each potato so that they will stand upright in a dish.

Using a spoon or a melon baller, scoop out a small cavity in each potato. Fill the cavities with sour cream and top with caviar. Serve warm or chilled.

serves 6 to 8

■ Spinach Pâté

1¼ pounds (550 grams) fresh spinach
boiling water
¾ cup (6 fl oz or 180 ml) heavy cream
  (single cream)
3 large eggs
4 ounces (120 grams) tuna fish packed in
  olive oil, drained and flaked
4 anchovy fillets, drained
½ cup (120 grams) finely chopped scallions
  (green onions)
1 tablespoon fresh lemon juice
⅓ cup (75 grams) soft fresh white bread
  crumbs
½ teaspoon salt
¼ teaspoon freshly ground black pepper

Preheat the oven to 375°F (190°C).

Generously butter the bottom of an 8½ × 4½ inch (21½ × 11½ cm) loaf pan. Line the bottom with waxed paper or parchment paper cut to size. Butter the paper.

Wash the spinach carefully to remove all grit. Discard any tough stems and discolored leaves. Place the spinach into a large saucepan and cover. Cook over medium heat for 3 to 4 minutes, or until the spinach is bright green and tender. Do not add water to the saucepan; the spinach will steam in the water clinging to its leaves from the washing.

Drain the spinach well. Squeeze it with your hands to remove as much moisture as possible. Chop the spinach coarsely and set aside in a large mixing bowl.

Put the heavy cream (single cream), eggs, tuna, anchovies, scallions and lemon juice into the container of a food processor or blender. Purée until the mixture is smooth. Transfer the mixture to the mixing bowl with the spinach and add the bread crumbs, salt and pepper. Mix well.

Turn the mixture into the prepared loaf pan and cover it with a piece of aluminum foil. Place the loaf pan into a larger baking dish. Pour the boiling water into the baking dish until there is enough to come halfway up the sides of the loaf pan.

Bake in the center of the oven for 1 hour or until a knife inserted into the center of the pâté comes out clean but not dry. Remove the pan from the oven and from the water bath. Place the loaf pan on a rack and cool to room temperature.

Refrigerate the pâté, covered, for 3 to 4 hours, or until it is well chilled. To serve, carefully unmold the pâté onto a serving plate and slice it thinly.

serves 8

■ Cheese Balls

12 ounces (340 grams) Brie cheese, at room
  temperature, rind discarded
½ cup (120 grams) sweet butter, softened
4 ounces (120 grams) fresh cream cheese,
  softened
2 tablespoons brandy
3 drops Tabasco sauce
½ teaspoon drained prepared white
  horseradish
salt to taste, if desired
freshly ground pepper to taste
5 ounces (150 grams) dark, dense
  pumpernickel bread, cubed

In the large bowl of an electric mixer, combine the Brie, butter, cream cheese, brandy, Tabasco sauce, horseradish, salt and pepper. Beat until smooth and well blended, about 2 minutes. Cover the bowl and chill for 4 hours or overnight.

Place the bread cubes into the container of a food processor or blender. Process until the cubes become fine crumbs.

Cover the bottom of a shallow dish with the bread crumbs.

With the hands, form the chilled cheese mixture into 1-inch (2½ cm) balls. Roll the balls in the bread crumbs until they are completely coated. Arrange the balls on a serving platter and serve them at room temperature.

serves 8 to 10

■ Chicken Liver Mousse

1½ cups (340 grams) sweet butter, softened
1 pound (450 grams) chicken livers
¼ cup (2 fl oz or 60 ml) Calvados or apple
 brandy
1 cup (225 grams) coarsely chopped shelled
 walnuts
salt to taste, if desired
freshly ground black pepper to taste

Melt ½ cup (120 grams) of the butter in a skillet over moderate heat. Add the livers and sauté gently until they are lightly browned but still pink inside, about 5 to 7 minutes. Remove the skillet from the heat and let the livers cool.

Put the cooled livers and the pan drippings, the remaining butter, Calvados and walnuts into the container of a food processor or blender. Process until the mixture is smooth and finely chopped.

Transfer the liver mixture to a bowl and season to taste with salt and pepper. Cover the mousse and chill for 4 hours or overnight. Serve with crackers or thinly sliced crusty bread.

serves 6 to 8

■ Pâté-Stuffed Mushrooms

¼ cup (60 grams) sweet butter
1 pound (450 grams) ground veal
½ cup (4 fl oz or 120 ml) golden rum
1 small onion, chopped
4 to 5 ounces (120 to 150 grams) liver pâté
1 cup (225 grams) chopped pitted (stoned)
 olives
3 tablespoons (45 grams) finely chopped
 chives
2 tablespoons drained capers
½ cup (120 grams) fine bread crumbs
salt to taste, if desired
24 large mushroom caps
capers for garnish

Heat the butter in a large skillet and sauté the veal with the rum and onions until the veal has lost its pink color and is cooked, about 10 minutes. Remove the skillet from the heat and let cool.

Put the veal mixture into the container of a food processor or blender. Add the liver pâté and process until smooth.

Fill the mushroom caps with the pâté mixture about 30 minutes before serving. Garnish with capers.

serves 6

■ Stuffed Chicken Slices

6 ounces (170 grams) bottled roasted red
 peppers
2 large whole chicken breasts, skinned and
 boned
8 whole scallions (green onions)
¼ cup (2 fl oz or 60 ml) soy sauce
2 tablespoons rice wine vinegar
2 teaspoons superfine sugar (castor sugar)

Drain the jar of roast peppers. Cut the roasted pepper pieces into thin strips.

Cut the chicken breasts in half. Place each half between two sheets of waxed paper. With a mallet or the side of a heavy knife or cleaver, gently pound the breast halves until they are flattened to about ¼ inch (1 cm) thick. Cut each breast half in half lengthwise.

Turn the cut side of each piece of chicken breast toward you as you work. Place 1 scallion on top of the chicken along the cut side and trim it if it protrudes beyond the chicken. Place a line of red pepper strips next to the scallion. Roll up the chicken into a jellyroll-like cylinder, starting with the cut side. Place the chicken cylinders, seam-side down, into a shallow dish.

In a small bowl combine the soy sauce, vinegar and sugar. Pour the mixture over the chicken cylinders and marinate for 30 minutes.

Carefully remove the chicken cylinders from the marinade and closely wrap each one individually in plastic wrap.

Arrange the cylinders on a rack or in a steamer in a large saucepan filled with 2 cups boiling water. Cover and steam the cylinders until firm, about 5 to 7 minutes. Remove the cylinders from the saucepan and cool. Chill for 4 hours or overnight.

When ready to serve, unwrap the cylinders and slice them diagonally into 1-inch (2½ cm) pieces. Arrange on a platter and serve.

serves 10 to 12

■ Chicken Wing Appetizer

3 pounds (1 kg 350 grams) chicken wings
½ cup (120 grams) sweet butter
1 cup (8 fl oz or 240 ml) soy sauce
1 cup (225 grams) firmly packed light brown sugar
¾ cup (6 fl oz or 180 ml) water
½ teaspoon dry mustard
¼ teaspoon cinnamon

Trim the tips from the chicken wings and cut the membrane between the first and second joints. Arrange the wings in a single layer in a large baking pan.

In a saucepan combine the butter, soy sauce, sugar, water, mustard and cinnamon. Cook over moderate heat until the butter melts and the sugar dissolves. Remove the saucepan from the heat and cool completely.

Pour the mixture over the chicken wings and marinate at room temperature for 2 to 2½ hours. Turn occasionally.

Preheat the oven to 375°F (190°C). Bake the wings for 1½ hours, turning every 20 minutes. Remove wings from the oven, drain briefly on paper towels, and serve.

serves 4 to 6

■ Smoked Salmon Squares

2 tablespoons (30 grams) sweet butter, softened
¾ teaspoon drained prepared white horseradish
6 thin slices square pumpernickel bread
6 ounces (180 grams) thinly sliced smoked salmon
48 capers, drained

In a small mixing bowl combine the butter and horseradish. Spread a thin layer of the mixture on each slice of bread.

Cover each slice of bread with a single layer of the smoked salmon. Cut each slice into 4 squares. Garnish each square with 2 capers and serve.

serves 6

■ Seviche

2 pounds (900 grams) fresh trout or any other firm white fish or scallops
juice of 3 limes
juice of 3 lemons
1 large sweet red pepper
1 large red onion, thinly sliced and separated into rings
2 canned jalapeño peppers, seeded and diced
salt to taste, if desired
freshly ground black pepper to taste
¾ cup (6 fl oz or 180 ml) olive oil

Slice the fish into strips approximately 4 × ½ inch (10 × 1½ cm) in size. Put the strips into a shallow dish and cover with the lime and lemon juice. Mix well, cover, and refrigerate for 4 hours.

Place the red pepper on a broiler pan and broil, turning often, until the pepper is blackened all over. Put the pepper into a paper bag and fold the bag closed. Let the pepper cool for 8 to 10 minutes. Remove it from the bag and rub off the skin, using your fingers. Seed and stem the pepper and cut it into thin strips.

Remove the fish from the refrigerator and discard the marinade. In a bowl (preferably glass) make layers of the fish, red onion rings, red pepper strips and jalapeño peppers. Salt and pepper each layer heavily.

Pour the olive oil over the bowl, cover, and chill. Serve as an appetizer or first course with thinly sliced bread.

serves 8

Soups

■ Swirled Corn Soup

as served at Trump's, Los Angeles, California

2 sweet red peppers
6 ears corn (sweet corn)
2 tablespoons (30 grams) sweet butter
2 medium-sized onions, coarsely chopped
2 cups (16 fl oz or 480 ml) chicken broth
1 cup (8 fl oz or 240 ml) heavy cream (single cream)
½ teaspoon salt, if desired

Put the peppers on a broiling pan and broil, turning often, until they are blackened all over. Put the peppers into a paper bag and fold it closed. Let the peppers cool for about 8 to 10 minutes. Remove the peppers from the bag and rub off the skin with your fingers. Remove the stems and seeds and chop the peppers coarsely.

Put the chopped peppers into the container of a food processor or blender. Process until the peppers are a smooth purée. Pour the purée through a fine sieve placed over a bowl. Discard any solids remaining in the sieve. Reserve the strained purée.

Using a small sharp knife, cut the kernels from the ears of corn. Scrape the cobs with the side of a spoon to remove the remaining kernels. There should be about 3 cups.

Melt the butter in a large saucepan over moderate heat. Add the onions and sauté until they are translucent but not brown, about 3 minutes. Add the corn and con-

tinue to sauté, stirring often, for 5 minutes or longer. Add the chicken broth, stir well, and cover the saucepan. Lower the heat and simmer for 15 minutes.

Remove the saucepan from the heat. A little at a time, put the soup into the container of a food processor or blender and process until it is a smooth purée. Pour the purée through a fine sieve over a bowl. Discard any solids remaining in the sieve and return the strained purée to the saucepan. Add the cream and cook over low heat, stirring constantly, for 5 minutes. Season the soup with salt and pepper and remove from the heat.

Ladle the soup into individual serving bowls. Using a spoon, swirl some of the red pepper purée across the top of each bowl. Serve hot or cold.

serves 6

■ Orange Carrot Soup

2 tablespoons (30 grams) sweet butter
4 carrots, thinly sliced
½ cup (120 grams) finely chopped onion
2 cups (16 fl oz or 480 ml) chicken broth
1 cup (8 fl oz or 240 ml) fresh orange juice
½ teaspoon freshly grated nutmeg
salt to taste, if desired
freshly ground black pepper to taste

Melt the butter over moderate heat in a saucepan. Add the carrots and onions and sauté until the onions begin to turn golden, about 5 minutes. Add the chicken broth and stir. Cover the saucepan and cook over low heat until the carrots are tender, about 20 minutes.

Strain the soup through a fine sieve. Reserve the liquid. Transfer the solids in the sieve to the container of a food processor or blender. Add ½ cup (4 fl oz or 120 ml) of the reserved liquid and purée until smooth.

Return the purée to the saucepan along with the rest of the reserved broth. Add the orange juice and nutmeg and salt and pepper to taste. Simmer over low heat until the soup is heated through. Serve hot.

serves 4

■ Double Mushroom Soup

as served by Barbara Faltz

2 ounces (60 grams) dried shiitake
  mushrooms
boiling water
2 tablespoons (30 grams) sweet butter
1 tablespoon olive oil
1 medium-sized onion, finely chopped
1 pound (450 grams) fresh mushrooms,
  thinly sliced
¼ cup (60 grams) flour (plain flour)
1 teaspoon salt, if desired
¼ teaspoon freshly ground black pepper
1 cup (8 fl oz or 240 ml) beef broth
1 cup (8 fl oz or 240 ml) chicken broth
¾ cup (6 fl oz or 180 ml) milk
½ cup (4 fl oz or 120 ml) heavy cream
  (single cream)
5 tablespoons dry sherry
2 tablespoons fresh lemon juice
½ cup (4 fl oz or 120 ml) sour cream or plain
  yogurt

Put the dried mushrooms in a bowl and add enough boiling water to cover. Soak the mushrooms until softened, about 1½ hours.

In a saucepan over moderate heat, melt the butter and oil together. Add the onions and sauté until soft, about 3 to 5 minutes. Stir occasionally. Add the fresh mushrooms. Cook, stirring frequently, until the mushrooms are soft, about 2 to 3 minutes. Add the flour, salt and pepper to the saucepan. Stir well to coat the mushrooms. Stir in the beef and chicken broths.

Drain the dried mushrooms well and reserve the soaking liquid. Strain the soaking liquid into a measuring cup. Add enough water to the liquid to make 2 cups (16 fl oz or 480 ml).

Add the soaking liquid to the saucepan. Add the soaked dried mushrooms and simmer gently for 12 to 15 minutes.

In batches, transfer the soup to the container of a food processor or blender. Process until it is a smooth purée.

Return the purée to the saucepan. Over moderate heat, bring it just to the boiling point, but do not allow it to boil. Stir in the milk, cream, sherry and lemon juice.

Serve hot or cold, garnished with sour cream or plain yogurt.

serves 4 to 6

■ Creamy Garlic Soup

6 tablespoons (90 grams) sweet butter
2 cups (480 grams) finely chopped onion
½ cup (120 grams) chopped garlic (about 35
  cloves)
½ cup (75 grams) flour (plain flour)
6 cups (2½ pints or 1.5 litres) chicken broth
1 cup (8 fl oz or 240 ml) dry vermouth
½ cup (4 fl oz or 120 ml) sour cream or plain
  yogurt
¼ teaspoon freshly grated nutmeg
chopped fresh chives

In a large saucepan over low heat, melt the butter. Add the onion and garlic and sauté, stirring frequently, until the onion is tender, about 10 minutes. Sprinkle the flour over the onions and garlic and stir. Cook, stirring constantly, for 3 to 4 min-

to 7 zucchini (courgette) slices from the saucepan and add them to the broth. Transfer the remaining zucchini (courgette) slices to the container of a food processor or blender and process to a smooth purée.

Add the broth and remaining zucchini (courgette) slices to the purée. Process briefly until the slices are finely chopped and the broth is blended into the purée, about 2 to 3 seconds.

Transfer the purée to a large bowl. Add the sherry and cream. Cover the bowl and chill for at least 4 hours or overnight. Add salt to taste and serve garnished with chopped chives.

serves 4 to 6

■ Coriander and Yogurt Soup

3 cups (675 grams) plain yogurt
2 cups (450 grams) loosely packed coriander
  leaves
½ cup (4 fl oz or 120 ml) milk
½ cup (120 grams) finely chopped scallion
  greens
1 tablespoon finely chopped fresh parsley
3 cups (24 fl oz or 720 ml) chicken broth
freshly ground black pepper to taste

In the container of a food processor or blender, combine the yogurt, coriander, milk, cream, scallion greens and parsley. Process until smooth, about 20 seconds.

Transfer the mixture to a large bowl. Add the chicken broth and stir until well blended. Refrigerate the soup for at least 6 hours or overnight.

Serve hot or cold, adding the pepper to taste. To serve the soup hot, put it in a saucepan and heat until just warmed through.

serves 8

■ Lime and Cucumber Soup

2 large cucumbers, peeled and seeded
½ cup (4 fl oz or 120 ml) milk
½ cup (4 fl oz or 120 ml) heavy cream
  (single cream)
1 cup (8 fl oz or 240 ml) sour cream
1 cup (8 fl oz or 240 ml) plain yogurt
finely grated peel of 3 limes
2 tablespoons fresh lime juice
2 tablespoons chopped fresh chives
1 tablespoon minced shallot
salt to taste, if desired
freshly ground black pepper to taste
chopped fresh chives for garnish

Coarsely grate the cucumbers into a large bowl. Add the milk, cream, sour cream, yogurt and lime peel. Mix well.

Add the lime juice, chives, shallots, salt and pepper. Stir until well blended. Cover the bowl and chill the soup for at least 4 hours or overnight.

Serve garnished with chopped chives.

serves 6 to 8

Salads

In the classic French cuisine a salad was invariably served after the main course, to cleanse the palate. It was equally invariably a simple green salad dressed with oil and vinegar, salt and pepper and sometimes a touch of mustard. The green salad was inviolate, the greens changing only with the seasons, and only occasionally enhanced with a touch of beetroot or a crouton or two.

No longer! Today a salad can be anything from a snack to a main course to an appetizer. It can be a combination of simple greens to a concoction of meat or fish with vegetables, fruits, nuts. It can be as primitive as peasant bread with garlic and olive oil or as complex as a Genoese Capon Magro with its multiple layers of fish, shellfish, vegetables, sauce and garnishes.

Whatever you serve as a salad, it must contain nothing but the freshest of ingredients. No wilted lettuce leaves, no watery tomatoes, no three-day-old leftovers. Any cooked ingredients should be cooked sparingly, *al dente*. Otherwise they will look wilted and gray. Also remember that any dressing will soften the ingredients through its marinating action. Likewise, tomatoes should be added at the last possible moment, as they will disperse their watery insides, diluting the dressing and leaving you with a pool of horrendous proportions at the bottom of the bowl.

What a salad is doused with is very much a matter of taste, but please use the very best possible oils and vinegars, and fresh herbs if possible. Pepper should always be freshly ground. Avoid any addition of sugar to the dressing. The matter of oils is always fraught with controversy. Suffice it to say that you should use the best olive oil you can afford. It is always a better choice than any much-promoted vegetable oil blend. Other oils such as sesame oil, walnut oil and hazelnut oil, have powerful flavors. Dark sesame oil is available in any Oriental market; walnut and hazelnut oil may take more searching in shops to find. All add a rich, deep flavor to salad dressings. Use them with discretion.

Vinegars come in many types and degrees of acidity. The mellow flavor of balsamic vinegar is worth seeking out. These vinegars are aged in wooden casks much as fine brandies are. Vinegars made from red or white wine, cider or malt are also good for dressing salads. Avoid distilled white vinegar—it is good only for pickling. Flavored vinegars, such as those made with tarragon, blueberries, raspberries or thyme, add a subtle touch to to salads. Lemon or lime juice can often be substituted for vinegar to good effect. Add vinegar or citrus juice with a sparing hand. Otherwise, the natural flavors of the ingredients will be overwhelmed.

Finally, whatever salad and dressing you choose, arrange it with a light hand and a discerning eye. It is the bouquet on the table.

■ Endive and Chicory (Escarole) Salad with Warm Bacon Dressing

4 Belgian endives
2 small heads chicory (escarole)
Warm Bacon Dressing:
½ pound (225 grams) slab bacon
4 tablespoons red wine vinegar
freshly ground black pepper to taste
salt to taste, if desired

Warm and gently dry the endives and the chicory (escarole). Tear them into bite-sized pieces and put them into a salad bowl.

Slice the bacon into ¼-inch (¾ cm) strips.

Cook the bacon in a skillet over medium heat until it is crisp and well browned, about 5 minutes. Drain well on paper towels. Reserve 2 tablespoons of the bacon drippings.

in the salad bowl, toss the greens with the vinegar and season them with pepper. Add the bacon and the bacon drippings; toss again. Season with additional salt and pepper if desired. Serve at once.

serves 4

■ Watercress and Endive Salad with Light Vinaigrette

4 Belgian endives
1 bunch watercress
¼ cup (60 grams) pomegranate seeds
1 large whole scallion
Light Vinaigrette:
1 tablespoon red wine vinegar
2 tablespoons light olive oil
salt to taste, if desired
freshly ground black pepper to taste

Wash and gently dry the watercress and endives. Remove any tough stems and blemished leaves from the watercress. Cut the endive into 1-inch (2½ cm) pieces.

Put the greens into a large bowl.

Trim the scallion and slice it, green part included, into very thin pieces. Reserve.

In a small mixing bowl combine the vinegar, oil, salt and pepper. Whisk until smooth and well blended.

Season the watercress and endive with additional salt and pepper. Add the scallion and toss well.

Pour the dressing over the salad and toss well. Adjust the seasonings to taste.

Distribute the salad on individual serving plates and top each serving with 1 tablespoon pomegranate seeds. Serve at once.

serves 4

■ Italian Greens with Mustard Vinaigrette

½ head romaine (cos) lettuce
1 bunch arugala (rocket) or watercress
1 head radicchio or Belgian endive
Mustard Vinaigrette:
6 tablespoons olive oil
2 tablespoons white wine vinegar
1 teaspoon white wine vinegar
1 teaspoon Dijon-style mustard
½ teaspoon finely chopped garlic
½ teaspoon ground salt, if desired
freshly ground black pepper to taste

Wash and gently dry the romaine, arugala (rocket) and radicchio. Tear the romaine and radicchio into bite-sized pieces; trim the stems from the arugala (rocket). Put the greens into a large salad bowl.

In a small mixing bowl combine the vinegar, mustard, garlic, salt and pepper. Whisk together until well blended. In a slow, steady stream, whisk in the olive oil. Continue whisking until vinaigrette is smooth.

Toss the greens with the vinaigrette and serve.

serves 4

■ Cucumber and Watercress Salad with Hazelnut Oil Dressing

2 cups (16 fl oz or 480 ml) cold water
2 tablespoons coarse salt
1½ pounds (675 grams) thin cucumber
3 bunches watercress
Hazelnut Oil Dressing:
⅓ cup (3 fl oz or 75 ml) red wine vinegar
2 teaspoons Dijon-style mustard
⅓ cup (3 fl oz or 75 ml) hazelnut oil
½ cup (4 fl oz or 120 ml) light olive oil
2 tablespoons chopped fresh chives
salt to taste, if desired
freshly ground black pepper to taste

Put the water into a large glass, ceramic or plastic (not metal!) bowl. Stir in the salt. Continue stirring until the salt is dissolved.

Slice the cucumbers very thinly and add them to the salt water. Soak for 1 hour.

Drain the cucumbers and rinse under cold running water. Drain well again. Wrap the cucumbers in a clean cotton kitchen or tea towel and squeeze out any additional water.

Wash and gently dry the watercress. Discard any tough stems and blemished leaves. Arrange the watercress on a flat serving platter. Top the watercress with the cucumber slices.

In a small mixing bowl combine the vinegar and mustard. Whisk to blend. In a slow, steady stream, whisk in the hazelnut oil and the olive oil. Continue whisking until the dressing is smooth and well blended. Whisk in the chives, salt and pepper. Pour the dressing over the salad and serve.

serves 8 to 10

■ Spinach and Mushroom Salad

1 pound (450 grams) fresh spinach
8 large mushrooms
Dressing:
2 tablespoons water
1 crushed garlic clove
1 finely chopped whole scallion (green onion)
¼ teaspoon dried basil
¼ teaspoon ground cumin
¼ teaspoon dried oregano
salt to taste, if desired
¾ cup (6 fl oz or 180 ml) olive oil
7 teaspoons white wine vinegar

Carefully wash the spinach to remove all grit. Discard any tough stems and blemished leaves.

Wipe the mushrooms clean with a damp paper towel. Remove the stems and discard. Cut the caps into thin slices. Put the mushroom slices into a large salad bowl.

Tear the spinach into bite-sized pieces and put them on top of the mushrooms in the salad bowl.

In a small mixing bowl, combine the water, garlic, scallion, basil, cumin, oregano and salt. Whisk until well blended. Add the olive oil and vinegar and whisk again until well blended.

Pour the dressing over the spinach and mushrooms. Let the dressing collect in the bottom of the bowl. Wait 3 minutes while the mushrooms marinate briefly in the dressing. Toss gently and serve.

serves 4

■ Summer Squash Salad

2 medium-sized onions
¾ pound (340 grams) zucchini (courgette)
¾ pound (340 grams) yellow summer squash
¼ cup (2 fl oz or 60 ml) olive oil
1 garlic clove, minced
1 large ripe tomato
10 oil-cured black olives
1 tablespoon chopped fresh parsley
salt to taste, if desired
freshly ground black pepper to taste
2 tablespoons fresh lemon juice
4 large chicory (escarole) leaves

Peel and quarter the onions. Cut each quarter into thin slices.

Wash and trim the zucchinis (courgettes) and yellow squash. Cut each squash lengthwise into quarters. Cut each quarter into thin slices.

In a large skillet, heat the olive oil until it is very hot. Add the onion and garlic. Lower the heat and sauté until the onion is soft but not brown, about 8 minutes. Stir often.

Add the zucchini (courgette) and yellow squash slices to the skillet. Stir until slices are thoroughly coated with the olive oil. Cover the skillet and cook over low heat, stirring occasionally, until the squash is tender but still firm, about 10 minutes. Remove the skillet from the heat and uncover.

Peel, quarter, and seed the tomato.

Halve the olives and remove the pits. Add the tomato, olives, parsley, salt and pepper to the skillet holding the squash. Stir until the ingredients are well blended. Transfer the mixture to a serving bowl and allow it to cool to room temperature.

When ready to serve, add the lemon juice and stir well. Line 4 individual serving plates with the chicory (escarole) leaves and top with the salad.

serves 4

■ Fennel Salad

1 medium-sized fennel
4 radishes, thinly sliced
2 seedless oranges, peeled and sectioned
4 black olives, pitted (stoned) and halved
4 tablespoons minced onion
several torn feathers from fennel
Dressing:
6 tablespoons olive oil
3 tablespoons cider vinegar
1 teaspoon Pernod or other anise-flavored
  liqueur
salt to taste, if desired
cayenne pepper to taste

Slice the bulb and stalk of the fennel into rings and put them into a salad bowl. Arrange the radish slices, orange sections, olives, onion and torn fennel feathers over the fennel rings.

In a small mixing bowl combine the olive oil, vinegar, Pernod, salt and cayenne pepper. Whisk until well blended. Pour over the salad and serve.

serves 4

■ Three-Greens Salad with Hot Cheese Dressing

1 medium head curly escarole (chicory)
2 small heads Boston lettuce or any soft
  lettuce
1 medium-sized head romaine (cos) lettuce
Hot Cheese Dressing:
½ cup (4 fl oz or 120 ml) olive oil
4 teaspoons minced shallot
2 teaspoons finely chopped garlic
½ cup (4 fl oz or 120 ml) red wine vinegar
2 tablespoons fresh lemon juice
4 teaspoons Dijon-style mustard
freshly ground black pepper to taste
10 ounces (280 grams) ripe Brie cheese

Remove the rind from the Brie and cut the cheese into small pieces. Allow the cheese to come to room temperature and soften.

Wash and gently dry all the lettuces. Tear them into bite-sized pieces and put them into a large salad bowl.

In a large skillet, heat the olive oil over very low heat until warm, about 8 to 10 minutes. Add the shallots and garlic and cook, stirring often, until the shallots are transparent, about 5 minutes. Add the vinegar, lemon juice and mustard. Mix well to blend. Add the Brie and stir constantly until the mixture is smooth. Season the dressing with pepper to taste.

Toss the salad with the hot dressing and serve at once.

serves 8

■ Broccoli and Red Pepper with Vinaigrette

2 sweet red peppers
6 cups (1.35 kg) broccoli flowerettes
Vinaigrette:
2 tablespoons fresh lemon juice
1 teaspoon Dijon-style mustard
6 tablespoons olive oil
salt to taste, if desired
freshly ground black pepper to taste

Preheat the broiler to high.

Place the red peppers on a broiler pan and broil, turning often, until the peppers are blackened all over. Put the peppers into a paper bag and fold the bag closed. Let the peppers cool for 8 to 10 minutes. Remove them from the bag and rub off the skins, using your fingers. Seed and stem the peppers and cut them into long thin strips. Put the strips into a bowl, cover, and chill for 4 hours or overnight.

Cook the broccoli flowerettes for 2 minutes in a saucepan of boiling water. Drain well and rinse the broccoli under cold running water. Drain well again and gently dry the broccoli. Place the broccoli into a large bowl, cover, and chill for 4 hours or overnight.

In a small mixing bowl combine the lemon juice, mustard, salt and pepper. Blend well. In a slow, steady stream, whisk in the olive oil. Continue to whisk until the vinaigrette is smooth.

Add the red pepper strips to the bowl holding the broccoli. Pour the vinaigrette over the mixture and toss well. Serve at once.

serves 4 to 6

■ Avocado and Papaya Salad with Mango Dressing

1 large head leafy lettuce
2 large ripe avocados, peeled and quartered
2 ripe papayas, peeled and quartered
1 small red onion, thinly sliced
Mango Dressing:
1 extremely ripe mango
2 tablespoons dry vermouth
1 tablespoon chopped fresh mint
salt to taste, if desired
freshly ground black pepper to taste
¾ cup (6 fl oz or 180 ml) light olive oil

Wash and gently dry the lettuce. Arrange a layer of lettuce on 8 individual.

Thinly slice the avocado and papaya quarters. Separate the onion slices into rings. Arrange slices of avocado and papaya on top of the lettuce on the serving plates; arrange onion rings on top of the avocado and papaya. Chill the plates.

Squeeze the mango in your hands to soften it. Cut off one end. Squeeze the mango over a small mixing bowl until all the juice has been removed.

Add the vermouth, mint, salt and pepper to the mango juice. In a slow, steady stream, whisk in the oil. Continue to whisk until the dressing is smooth and well blended. Allow the dressing to stand at room temperature for 1 hour before using. Whisk before using.

To serve, remove the plates from the refrigerator. Spoon the dressing over each salad and serve at once.

serves 8

Roquefort Dressing

¼ cup (2 fl oz or 60 ml) white wine vinegar
salt to taste, if desired
freshly ground black pepper to taste
½ cup (4 fl oz or 120 ml) olive oil
2 tablespoons heavy cream (single cream)
¼ cup (60 grams) crumbled Roquefort or
    blue cheese
3 drops fresh lemon juice

In a small mixing bowl combine the vinegar, salt and pepper. Whisk together until well blended.

In a slow, steady stream, whisk in the olive oil. Whisk in the cream. Continue to whisk until the dressing is smooth and well blended. Add the crumbled cheese and lemon juice. Stir briefly and serve.

makes 1 cup (8 fl oz or 240 ml)

Touch of Asia Dressing

2 teaspoons water
2 teaspoons soy sauce
½ teaspoon sesame oil
1 garlic clove, crushed
freshly ground black pepper to taste
¾ cup (6 fl oz or 180 ml) olive oil
7 teaspoons rice wine vinegar

In a small mixing bowl combine the water, soy sauce, sesame oil, garlic and black pepper. Whisk together until well blended.

In a slow, steady stream, whisk in the olive oil. Continue to whisk until the dressing is smooth and well blended. Let stand for at least 2 minutes.

Whisk in the vinegar and serve.

makes 1¼ cups (10 fl oz or 300 ml)

Walnut Vinaigrette

½ cup (120 grams) chopped walnuts
4 tablespoons red wine vinegar
4 tablespoons balsamic vinegar
½ teaspoon salt

¼ teaspoon freshly ground black pepper
1 cup (8 fl oz or 240 ml) walnut oil
¼ cup (2 fl oz or 60 ml) olive oil

Preheat the oven to 350°F (180°C).

Place the chopped walnuts in a shallow baking dish and toast in the oven for 5 minutes. Remove from the oven and let walnuts cool in the dish.

In a small mixing bowl combine the red wine vinegar, balsamic vinegar, salt and pepper. Whisk together until well blended.

In a slow, steady stream, whisk in the olive oil. Continue to whisk until the vinaigrette is smooth and well blended. Add the walnuts, whisk gently, and serve.

makes 1 cup (8 fl oz or 240 ml)

Basic Vinaigrette Dressing

¼ cup (2 fl oz or 60 ml) red wine vinegar
¾ cup (6 fl oz or 180 ml) olive oil
1 teaspoon Dijon-style mustard
½ teaspoon salt
¼ teaspoon freshly ground black pepper

In a small bowl, combine the vinegar, mustard, salt and pepper. Whisk together until well blended.

In a slow, steady stream, whisk in the olive oil. Continue to whisk until the vinaigrette is smooth and well blended.

makes ½ cup (4 fl oz or 120 ml)

Tangy Yogurt Dressing

½ cup (4 fl oz or 120 ml) plain yogurt
½ teaspoon prepared white horseradish,
    drained
1 tablespoon Dijon-style mustard
½ teaspoon ground cumin
1 teaspoon freshly grated lemon peel
salt to taste, if desired
freshly ground black pepper to taste

In a small mixing bowl combine the yogurt, horseradish, mustard, cumin, lemon peel, salt and pepper. Whisk until well blended, and serve.

makes ¾ cup (6 fl oz or 180 ml)

■ Balsamic Vinaigrette

1 shallot, finely chopped
1 teaspoon Dijon-style mustard
1½ tablespoons red wine vinegar
2 teaspoons balsamic vinegar
6 tablespoons olive oil
salt to taste, if desired
freshly ground black pepper to taste

In a small bowl, combine the shallot, mustard, red wine vinegar and balsamic vinegar. Whisk together until well blended.

In a slow, steady stream, whisk in the olive oil. Continue to whisk until the vinaigrette is smooth and well blended. Season to taste with salt and pepper and whisk gently.

makes ½ cup (4 fl oz or 120 ml)

■ Chinese Dressing

1 tablespoon water
2 teaspoons soy sauce
2 teaspoons oyster sauce
1 garlic clove, crushed
¼ teaspoon crumbled dried basil
¾ cup (6 fl oz or 180 ml) olive oil
7 teaspoons rice wine vinegar

In a small mixing bowl combine the water, soy sauce, oyster sauce, garlic and basil. Whisk together until well blended. Let stand for 3 minutes.

In a slow, steady stream, whisk in the olive oil. Whisk in the vinegar. Continue to whisk until the dressing is smooth and well blended, and serve.

makes 1½ cups (12 fl oz or 360 ml)

Composed Salads

■ Salmon Salad

as served at the Acute Café, New York

6 tablespoons raspberry vinegar
3 tablespoons finely chopped shallots
¾ cup (6 fl oz or 180 ml) olive oil
salt to taste, if desired
freshly ground black pepper to taste
½ pound (225 grams) salmon fillet, thinly sliced
¼ cup (2 fl oz or 60 ml) clarified butter (see page 123)
2 small heads Boston lettuce or any soft lettuce, washed and dried

In a small mixing bowl combine the vinegar and shallots. In a slow, steady stream, whisk in the olive oil. Continue to whisk until well blended. Add the salt and pepper and whisk again. Set aside.

Melt the butter in a large skillet over high heat. Sauté the salmon briefly for only 8 to 10 seconds on each side. Remove skillet from the heat.

Arrange the lettuce leaves on a large serving platter. Arrange the salmon slices on the lettuce. Whisk the dressing again and pour it evenly over the salmon. Serve while still warm.

serves 4

■ Fruit and Mussel Salad

as served at the Oyster Bar and Restaurant, New York, New York

40 scrubbed, rinsed and debearded fresh
    mussels
½ cup (4 fl oz or 120 ml) water
½ cup (4 fl oz or 120 ml) dry white wine
Dressing:
1 hard-cooked egg, finely chopped
1 egg yolk
3 tablespoons Dijon-style mustard
1 tablespoon finely chopped onion
2 teaspoons minced shallot
2 teaspoons chopped fresh basil or 1 teaspoon
    dried
2 teaspoons chopped fresh oregano or 1
    teaspoon dried
1 garlic clove, finely chopped
½ teaspoon salt
freshly ground black pepper to taste
3 tablespoons dry white wine
3 tablespoons white wine vinegar
1 cup (8 fl oz or 240 ml) olive oil
2 small heads Boston lettuce or any soft
    lettuce, washed and dried
2 ripe pears, peeled, cored and halved
watercress for garnish (optional)

Combine the water and white wine in a large pot. Bring to a boil and add the mussels. Cover the pot and cook, shaking the pot occasionally, until the mussels open, about 5 minutes. Remove the pot from the heat and cool. When the mussels are cool enough to handle, remove them from their shells. Remove the black rims if desired. Put the mussels into a large mixing bowl and set aside.

In a small bowl combine the hard-cooked egg, egg yolk, mustard, onion, shallot, basil, oregano, garlic, salt and pepper. Add the wine and vinegar. Whisk until well blended. In a slow, steady stream, whisk in the olive oil. Continue to whisk until the dressing is smooth and well blended.

Pour the dressing over the mussels and toss until well coated.

Line 4 individual serving plates with the lettuce leaves. Put half a pear on each plate. Spoon the mussels over the pears and serve. Garnish with watercress.
serves 4

■ Warm Scallop Salad

2 ripe tomatoes
⅓ cup (3 fl oz or 80 ml) olive oil
2 shallots, finely chopped
2 tablespoons fresh lime juice
½ teaspoon salt
½ teaspoon freshly ground black pepper
2 tablespoons finely chopped fresh basil or ½
    teaspoon dried
1 pound (450 grams) sea scallops
2 tablespoons olive oil
salt to taste, if desired
freshly ground black pepper to taste
2 bunches arugala (rocket), stems removed

Peel, halve, and seed the tomato. Chop it finely and set aside.

Heat ⅓ cup (3 fl oz or 80 ml) olive oil in a skillet over medium heat. Add the shallots and sauté until soft, about 2 to 3 minutes. Stir in the lime juice, salt and pepper. Remove the skillet from the heat and add the tomato and basil. Stir well and set the dressing aside.

Rinse and gently dry the scallops. Cut very large scallops in half.

Heat 2 tablespoons olive oil in another skillet over moderately high heat. Add the scallops and sauté, turning frequently, for 3 to 5 minutes. Remove the skillet from the heat and put the scallops into a large mixing bowl.

Add half the dressing to the warm scallops. Season with additional salt and pepper and toss well.

Distribute the arugala (rocket) evenly among 4 individual serving plates. Top each plate with a portion of the warm scallops. Drizzle additional dressing over each portion and serve.
serves 4

■ Lobster Salad

as served by Lionel Martinez

1½ cups (340 grams) coarsely chopped
   cooked lobster meat)
½ pound (225 grams) fresh mushrooms,
   sliced
2 cups (450 grams) fresh raspberries
Dressing:
6 tablespoons olive oil
2 tablespoons white wine vinegar
2 tablespoons Dijon-style mustard
2 tablespoons plain yogurt
1 teaspoon crushed dried mint
salt to taste, if desired
freshly ground black pepper to taste
4 large lettuce leaves, washed and dried

In a large bowl, combine the lobster meat, mushrooms and raspberries. Mix well and chill for 1 hour.

In a small mixing bowl combine the olive oil, vinegar, mustard, yogurt, mint, salt and pepper. Whisk until the dressing is well blended. Adjust seasonings to taste.

Arrange the lettuce leaves on 4 individual serving plates. Top each plate with a portion of the lobster mixture. Spoon the dressing over the salad and serve.
serves 4

■ Crabmeat Salad with Hot Caper Dressing

5 cups (1.125 kg) romaine (cos) lettuce, torn
   into bite-sized pieces
1 cup (225 grams) warm cooked crabmeat
Caper Dressing:
½ cup (4 fl oz or 120 ml) olive oil
3 tablespoons red wine vinegar
3 tablespoons drained capers
1 garlic clove, finely chopped
salt to taste, if desired
½ teaspoon dried oregano
freshly ground black pepper to taste

Place the romaine lettuce and the crabmeat in a salad bowl. Set aside.

In a saucepan combine the olive oil, vinegar, capers, garlic, salt, oregano and pepper. Heat just to the boiling point.

Pour the dressing over the lettuce and crabmeat. Toss well and serve at once.
serves 4

■ Veal Salad with Walnut Dressing

3 pounds (1.135 kg) boneless veal shoulder
2 carrots, cut into 2-inch (5 cm) pieces
2 celery stalks, cut into 2-inch (5 cm) pieces
3 unpeeled onions, quartered
8 sprigs parsley
4 unpeeled garlic cloves
10 whole black peppercorns
1¼ teaspoons salt
Walnut Dressing:
½ cup (4 fl oz or 120 ml) walnut oil
⅓ cup (75 grams) coarsely chopped walnuts
2 tablespoons white wine vinegar
1 teaspoon finely chopped drained green
   peppercorns
2 ripe avocados

Put the veal, carrots, celery, onions, parsley, garlic, black peppercorns and ½ teaspoon salt into a large pot. Add enough water to cover. Simmer, covered, over medium-low heat until the veal is tender, about 2 to 2½ hours.

When the veal is done, remove it from the pot. (Use the liquid and vegetables remaining in the pot for stock or discard.) When the veal is cool enough to handle, pull the meat apart into pieces that are about ½ × 2 inches (1½ × 5 cm) in size.

Put the veal pieces into a large mixing bowl. Add ½ teaspoon of salt and 2 tablespoons of walnut oil. Toss well until veal is coated and set aside.

Heat 1 tablespoon of the walnut oil in a small skillet. Add the walnuts and cook, stirring constantly, until browned, about 3 to 4 minutes. Remove skillet from heat and set aside.

In a small mixing bowl, combine the remaining walnut oil, vinegar, green peppercorns and remaining salt. Whisk together until the dressing is well blended

Peel the avocados. Cut them in half and remove the center pits. Cut each half into 6 long slices. Add the avocado slices to the dressing and toss.

Arrange the veal in the center of a serving platter. Top the avocado with the browned walnuts. Spoon the dressing over the entire salad and serve.

serves 4

■ Cold Beef Salad

2 pounds (900 grams) shell steak or entrecôte
salt to taste, if desired
freshly ground black pepper to taste
2 sweet red peppers, julienned
1 green pepper, julienned
10 whole scallions, thinly sliced
1½ cups (340 grams) mayonnaise
2 garlic cloves, finely chopped
1 teaspoon drained prepared white
    horseradish
1 head red leaf lettuce or any other lettuce,
    washed and dried
1 bunch watercress, tough stems removed,
    for garnish

Preheat the broiler or prepare the cooker for grilling.

Season the steak on both sides with salt and pepper to taste. Broil or grill the steak until it is medium rare, about 7 to 10 minutes per side. When done, remove the steak from the broiler or grill and cool completely. When cool, cut the steak into thin strips.

In a large bowl, combine the steak strips, red pepper, green pepper, scallions, mayonnaise, garlic and horseradish. Season with salt and pepper to taste and toss until all the ingredients are well coated. Cover the bowl and chill for 4 hours. Remove the salad from the refrigerator 30 minutes before serving.

Arrange the lettuce leaves on 4 individual serving plates. Place a portion of the salad on each plate. Garnish with watercress and serve.

serves 4

■ Warm Sweetbreads Salad

2 pounds (900 grams) sweetbreads
salt to taste, if desired
2 tablespoons olive oil
1½ pounds (675 grams) fresh spinach
4 ounces (120 grams) fresh green beans
    (French beans)
vegetable oil
4 large mushrooms, quartered and thinly
    sliced
Dressing:
6 tablespoons red wine vinegar
2 shallots, finely chopped
salt to taste, if desired
freshly ground black pepper to taste
¾ cup (6 fl oz or 180 ml) olive oil

Soak the sweetbreads in a bowl with enough cold water to cover for 2 hours. Change the water 3 times during this period.

Put the sweetbreads into a saucepan and cover with lightly salted water. Bring the water to a simmer and gently cook the sweetbreads over very low heat for 18 to 20 minutes. Remove the sweetbreads from the saucepan and put them into a bowl with ice water to cover. Cool for 5 to 7 minutes and drain well.

Remove any membranes or connecting tissues attached to the sweetbreads. Place the sweetbreads between two sheets of waxed paper. Place a large plate with a heavy tin on it on top of the sweetbreads. Refrigerate with the weight for 3 to 4 hours.

Cut the sweetbreads into thin slices. Gently pat the slices dry and season them with salt and pepper.

Heat the olive oil in a skillet. Add the spinach. Cover and cook until the spinach is just wilted, about 1 to 2 minutes. Season with salt and pepper and remove the skillet from the heat.

Cook the green beans (French beans) in a saucepan of boiling water until they are just tender, about 8 to 10 minutes. Drain well and rinse with cold water. Drain well again.

In another skillet, heat a layer of vegetable oil that is ⅛ inch (½ cm) deep. When the oil is very hot, sauté the sweetbread slices until golden, about 2 minutes. Turn frequently.

Using a slotted spoon, transfer the spinach from the skillet to a serving platter. Arrange the sautéed sweetbread slices on top of the spinach. Arrange the string beans (French beans) and mushroom slices on top of the sweetbreads.

In a small mixing bowl, combine the vinegar, shallots, salt and pepper. In a slow, steady stream, whisk in ¾ cup (6 fl oz or 180 ml) olive oil. Continue to whisk until the dressing is well blended.

Spoon the dressing over the salad and serve.

serves 4

■ Curried Apricot Chicken Salad

4 chicken breasts, skinned and boned
4 tablespoons (60 grams) sweet butter
1 cup (8 fl oz or 240 ml) plain yogurt
⅛ cup (30 grams) curry powder
salt to taste, if desired
freshly ground black pepper to taste
½ pound (225 grams) seedless green grapes
2 cups (450 grams) julienned dried apricots
2 cups (450 grams) drained mandarin orange
*   sections*
1 cup (225 grams) cashews or walnuts
½ cup (4 fl oz or 120 ml) apricot liqueur
1 head leafy lettuce, washed and dried

Cut the chicken breasts into 1-inch (2.5) cubes.

Melt the butter in a large skillet. Add the chicken and cook over moderately low heat, turning often, until the cubes are firm but not brown, about 7 to 10 minutes. Transfer the chicken, using a slotted spoon, to a mixing bowl.

In a small bowl, combine the yogurt and curry powder. Mix well. Add the mixture to the chicken. Season with salt and pepper and more curry, if desired.

Add the grapes, apricots, mandarin orange sections, cashews and apricot liqueur to the chicken. Toss until all the ingredients are well coated. Chill for at least 1 hour.

Line a serving dish with the lettuce leaves. Mound the salad on the lettuce and serve. Garnish with additional fruit if desired.

serves 4 to 6

■ Sliced Stuffed Breast of Chicken Salad

as served at Michael's, Los Angeles, California

2 whole chicken breasts, with wings

4 ounces (120 grams) softened fresh goat cheese (chèvre)

1½ tablespoons softened sweet butter

¼ teaspoon dried thyme

salt to taste, if desired

freshly ground black pepper to taste

10 fresh basil leaves, finely chopped

10 sprigs fresh coriander (cilantro), finely chopped

2 tablespoons finely chopped chives

2 tablespoons olive oil

4 cups (900 grams) mixed salad greens

2 sweet red peppers, julienned

Tomato Vinaigrette:

6 tablespoons olive oil

1 finely chopped shallot

1 crushed garlic clove

2 tablespoons white wine vinegar

salt to taste, if desired

freshly ground black pepper to taste

2 large tomatoes peeled, seeded and coarsely chopped

leaves from 2 sprigs coriander (cilantro)

Preheat the oven to 350°F (180°C).

With a small, sharp knife, bone the chicken breasts, leaving the skin and wings attached. Using the knife or your fingers, carefully make a pocket in each piece of chicken between the skin and the breast. Make the opening to the pocket as small as possible.

In a small mixing bowl combine the goat cheese, 1 tablespoon butter, the thyme, and salt and pepper to taste. Add all but ¼ teaspoon of the chopped basil, coriander and chives to the mixture and blend well. Set aside the reserved herbs for the vinaigrette.

Stuff the pockets in the chicken breasts with the goat cheese mixture.

Heat the 2 tablespoons olive oil and the remaining butter together in a skillet.

When the butter has melted, add the chicken breasts, skin-side down. Sauté, turning once, until the chicken is golden brown, about 8 minutes.

Put the chicken breasts into a baking dish large enough to hold them all in one layer. Bake for 5 to 7 minutes. Remove from the oven and cool in the dish for 10 to 12 minutes.

In a small mixing bowl, combine the 6 tablespoons of olive oil, shallots, garlic, vinegar, salt, pepper and the reserved chopped herbs. Whisk until smooth and well blended. Stir in the chopped tomatoes and coriander leaves.

Arrange the salad greens on 4 individual serving plates. Slice the chicken breasts at an angle, leaving the wings intact. Arrange the breast slices on the plates. Surround the slices with the red pepper strips. Spoon the dressing over the slices and the greens. Serve at once.

serves 4

Meatless Entrées

As people eat less and less meat, dairy products are coming more into their own as solid protein sources at little cost. Milk, cheese, yogurt, eggs, butter and cream need not be served plain. They can be combined or elaborated upon into literally thousands of delicious combinations.

Use yogurt instead of mayonnaise, or combine it with mayonnaise to create lighter-tasting salad dressings. Use milk instead of cream to create less fattening cream sauces. Butter can be combined with various oils to cut cholesterol as well as to keep the butter from burning.

Eggs are certainly the most versatile food in the kitchen. Whether poached, fried, scrambled, baked or boiled, they can create the basis for many dishes. They can be combined in soufflés, flans, omelettes and sauces. They are the save-all for unexpected company and quick and scrumptious lunches or late suppers. They combine with and accept all sorts of flavors.

Cheeses, likewise, need not be left to moulder on the cheeseboard. A *crotin*—a small goat cheese—melted over crisp salad greens, a Roquefort fritter, a soufflé, even a Welsh rarebit can, treated with discernment, form a splendid course in the most formal of meals.

No matter what dairy products you utilize in the kitchen, be sure they are as fresh as can be. This is especially true of the ones we do not think about too carefully. Freshly laid eggs are so superior to the eggs from the market dairy case that one taste will convert you forever. Likewise, butter at its best is a perfect accompaniment to prosciutto or good salami, and not merely a spread for inferior breads. The best advice is to experiment. You'll find a new world of taste temptations awaits you.

Carrot Soup

Potato and Zucchini (Courgette) Soup and Swirled Corn Soup (previous page)

Fresh Mozzarella with Tomatoes and Basil

Baked Whole Garlic

Roast Corn (Sweet Corn) with Herb Butter

smooth and well blended, about 2 minutes. Add the eggs and process for 2 to 3 seconds more. Add the cheese mixture to the mixing bowl with the basil mixture. Blend well.

Pour the mixture into the prepared springform pan and sprinkle with the pine nuts. Place the pan on a flat baking sheet. Bake for 1 hour and 15 minutes. Turn off the oven and allow the cheesecake to cool in the oven, with the door ajar, for 1 hour longer.

Remove the springform pan from the oven and put it on a cooling rack. Remove the sides from the pan and serve the cheesecake, sliced into wedges, at room temperature.

serves 10 to 12

■ Baked Goat Cheese (*Chèvre*) with Green Sauce

as adapted from Diane Rossen Worthington

2 tablespoons olive oil
¼ cup (60 grams) fresh breadcrumbs
½ pound (225 grams) goat cheese (chèvre)
½ pound (225 grams) fresh spinach
1 cup (225 grams) watercress leaves
boiling water
¼ cup (2 fl oz or 60 ml) vegetable oil
½ cup (4 fl oz or 120 ml) olive oil
¼ cup (2 fl oz or 60 ml) red wine vinegar
salt to taste, if desired
freshly ground black pepper to taste

Put the 2 tablespoons olive oil into a small bowl. Put the breadcrumbs into another small bowl.

With a sharp knife, divide the goat cheese into 4 equal wedges. Dip each wedge into the olive oil and then into the breadcrumbs. Turn the wedges to coat them evenly. Place the wedges into a shallow baking dish and refrigerate for 1½ hours.

Wash the spinach thoroughly to remove all grit. Discard any blemished leaves or tough stems. Plunge the spinach into a saucepan full of boiling water for 20 seconds. Drain well, rinse thoroughly with cold water, and drain well, again. Put the spinach into a clean kitchen towel and wring well to remove as much moisture as possible.

Plunge the watercress into a saucepan full of boiling water for 20 seconds. Drain well, rinse thoroughly with cold water, and drain well again. Put the watercress into a clean kitchen towel and wring well to remove as much liquid as possible.

Put the spinach, watercress, vegetable oil, olive oil, vinegar, salt and pepper into the container of a food processor or blender. Process for 30 to 40 seconds. Set the mixture aside.

Preheat the oven to 475°F (240°C).

Remove the baking dish with the goat cheese from the refrigerator and put it in the oven. Bake until the goat cheese is golden brown on the outside and soft on the inside, about 10 minutes.

To serve, gently spread the spinach and watercress mixture on a serving plate. Arrange the cheese wedges in the center of the plate and serve hot.

serves 4

■ Fresh Mozzarella with Tomatoes and Basil

½ pound (225 grams) fresh mozzarella cheese, thinly sliced
4 large ripe tomatoes, peeled and thinly sliced
¼ cup (60 grams) coarsely chopped fresh basil leaves
2 tablespoons Balsamic Vinaigrette (see page 25)

Arrange the mozzarella and tomato slices in overlapping circles on a serving platter. Sprinkle the cheese and tomatoes with the chopped basil.

Pour the balsamic vinaigrette over the cheese and tomatoes and serve.

serves 6

Fresh Mozzarella with Black Pepper

1 pound (450 grams) fresh or smoked
* mozzarella cheese*
⅓ cup (3 fl oz or 75 ml) olive oil
2 garlic cloves, crushed
1 teaspoon very coarsely ground black
* peppercorns*

Cut the mozzarella into ¼-inch (1 cm) slices. Arrange the slices on a serving plate.

In a small bowl combine the olive oil, garlic and peppercorns.

Spoon the oil and peppercorns mixture over the mozzarella. Cover the cheese completely. Let stand for 1 hour at room temperature before serving.

serves 6 to 8

Fried Mozzarella with Anchovy Sauce

4 thick slices fresh mozzarella cheese
flour seasoned with salt and pepper, for
* dredging*
1 large egg, beaten
⅔ cup (150 grams) fine breadcrumbs
6 tablespoons (90 grams) sweet butter
¼ cup (60 grams) drained capers
¼ cup (60 grams) rinsed and finely chopped
* anchovy fillets*
¼ cup (2 fl oz or 60 ml) dry white wine
4 thin lemon slices for garnish
watercress leaves for garnish

Put the seasoned flour, beaten egg, and breadcrumbs into separate small bowls.

Dip the mozzarella slices first in the flour and then in the egg. Roll the slices in the breadcrumbs to coat evenly. Put the coated slices on a rack.

Melt 2 tablespoons (30 grams) of the butter in a large skillet. When the butter is hot add the cheese slices and sauté over high heat until golden brown, about 1 to 2 minutes per side. Put the cooked slices

onto individual serving plates.

Add the anchovies, capers, wine and remaining butter to the skillet. Cook over medium heat, stirring constantly, until the butter melts.

Spoon the sauce over the mozzarella slices. Garnish each plate with a slice of lemon and some watercress leaves, if desired. Serve warm.

serves 4

Eggplant (Aubergine) and Pepper Soufflé

3 tablespoons (45 grams) sweet butter
2 large eggplants (aubergines)
1½ pounds (675 grams) sweet red peppers
½ cup (120 grams) ricotta cheese
2 tablespoons finely chopped coriander
* (cilantro)*
1 tablespoon minced green pepper
¼ teaspoon ground cumin
salt to taste, if desired
freshly ground black pepper to taste
¼ teaspoon cayenne pepper
8 egg yolks
8 egg whites

Preheat the oven to 400°F (200°C).

Generously butter 8 individual 10-ounce (300 ml) soufflé dishes. Refrigerate until needed.

Put the eggplants (aubergines) on a flat baking sheet and bake until soft, about 30 minutes. When done, remove from the oven and cut in half lengthwise. Let cool.

Roast the red peppers over an open flame or under the broiler until the skins are charred and black. Turn often. When blackened all over, put the peppers into a paper bag and close it. Let the peppers cool for 10 minutes. Remove them from the bag and rub off the skin with your fingers. Remove the seeds and cut the peppers into strips.

When the eggplants (aubergines) are cool enough to handle easily, scoop out the seeds and meat and put them into the container of a food processor or blender.

Add the red pepper strips, ricotta, coriander, green pepper, salt, pepper and cayenne. Process until the mixture is a smooth purée. Pour the purée into a large mixing bowl.

Whisk the egg yolks into the purée. Continue to whisk until well blended.

In a small bowl, beat the egg whites until they are stiff but not dry. Gently but quickly fold the egg whites into the purée.

Arrange the soufflé dishes on a flat baking sheet. Fill each dish to the rim with the soufflé mixture. Wipe away any overflow.

Bake soufflés until risen and browned, about 10 minutes. Serve at once.

serves 8

■ Mocha Café Soufflé

2 teaspoons sweet butter
⅔ cup (150 grams) sugar
⅓ cup (75 grams) unsweetened cocoa
¼ cup (60 grams) powdered instant espresso
3 tablespoons cornstarch
¾ cup (6 fl oz or 180 ml) milk
¼ cup (60 grams) sweet butter
1 teaspoon pure vanilla extract
4 egg yolk
4 egg whites
¼ teaspoon cream of tartar

Preheat the oven to 375°F (190°C).

Make a 2-inch (5 cm) collar for a 1½ quart (2½ pints or 1.5 litre) soufflé dish by folding a long piece of aluminum foil in half lengthwise. Lightly butter one side of the foil and wrap the foil around the dish, with the buttered side facing inward. Tie the collar in place with kitchen twine. Butter the inside of the dish with the remainder of the 2 teaspoons butter.

Combine ⅓ cup (75 grams) of the sugar with the cocoa, espresso powder and cornstarch in a saucepan. Add the milk and stir until smooth. Cook the mixture over moderate heat, stirring constantly, until thick and smooth. Remove the saucepan from the heat.

Add the vanilla and butter to the saucepan. Stir until the butter melts. Add the egg yolks, one at a time, beating well after each addition.

In a mixing bowl beat the egg whites until foamy. Add the cream of tartar and beat until well blended. Slowly sprinkle in the remaining ⅓ cup (75 grams) sugar. Continue to beat until the whites are stiff but not dry.

Stir one-quarter of the egg whites into the chocolate mixture, then pour the chocolate mixture back over the egg whites in the mixing bowl. Gently but quickly fold the mixtures together.

Pour the batter into the prepared soufflé dish and bake in the lower half of the oven for 25 to 35 minutes. The shorter baking time will result in a saucy center; the longer baking time will result in a firm center. Remove from the oven, remove the collar, and serve *immediately*.

serves 6

■ Goat Cheese (*Chèvre*) and Chives Soufflé

2 teaspoons sweet butter
2 tablespoons freshly gratead Parmesan cheese
4 tablespoons (60 grams) sweet butter
2 tablespoons (30 grams) flour (plain flour)
1 cup (8 fl oz or 240 ml) hot milk
½ teaspoon coarse salt
¼ teaspoon dry mustard
freshly ground black pepper to taste
¼ teaspoon cayenne pepper
4 egg yolks, lightly beaten
4 ounces (120 grams) cold, crumbled goat cheese
⅓ cup (75 grams) finely chopped fresh chives
6 egg whites

Preheat the oven to 425°F (220°C).

Make a 2-inch (5 cm) collar for a 1½ quart (2½ pints or 1.5 litre) soufflé dish by folding a long piece of aluminum foil in half lengthwise. lightly butter one side of the foil and wrap the foil around the dish, with the buttered side facing inward. Tie the collar in place with kitchen twine. Generously butter the inside of the soufflé dish with the remainder of the 2 teaspoons butter. Sprinkle the inside of the dish and the collar with the Parmesan cheese.

In a small saucepan, melt the butter. Add the flour and cook over low heat, stirring constantly, for 3 minutes. Gradually whisk in the milk. Continue to whisk constantly until the mixture is well-blended, smooth, thick and boiling, about 4 minutes. Remove the saucepan from the heat and add the salt, mustard, pepper and cayenne. Stir to mix well.

Beat the egg yolks lightly in a large mixing bowl. Slowly add ¼ cup (2 fl oz or 60 ml) of the hot milk mixture to the yolks. Stir well. Add the remaining milk mixture and stir until well blended. Add the goat cheese and chives. Stir until well blended.

In a small bowl beat the egg whites until they are stiff but not dry. Gently but quickly fold the egg whites into the egg yolk mixture.

Gently pour the batter into the prepared soufflé dish. Bake for 10 minutes. Lower the oven temperature to 375°F (190°C) and continue baking until the soufflé is risen and golden, about 20 minutes longer. Remove from the oven, remove the collar, and serve *immediately.*

serves 4 to 6

■ Apricot Soufflé

2 teaspoons sugar
6 ounces (180 grams) dried apricots
1 cup (8 fl oz or 240 ml) apple juice
6 large egg whites
¼ teaspoon salt
½ teaspoon cream of tartar
3 tablespoons (45 grams) sugar
1 teaspoon pure vanilla extract
whipped heavy cream (single cream)

Preheat the oven to 375°F (190°C).

Make a 2-inch (5 cm) collar for a 4-cup (1¾ pint or 1 litre) soufflé dish by folding a long piece of aluminum foil in half lengthwise. Lightly butter one side of the foil and wrap the foil around the dish, with the buttered side facing inward. Tie the collar in place with kitchen twine. Generously butter the inside of the soufflé dish with the remainder of the 2 teaspoons butter. Sprinkle the inside of the dish and collar with the 2 teaspoons sugar.

Put the dried apricots and apple juice into a saucepan. Bring the mixture to a boil. Reduce the heat and simmer, covered, until the apricots are soft, about 20 minutes.

Put the apricots and the cooking liquid into the container of a food processor or blender. Process until the mixture is a smooth purée. Pour the purée into a mixing bowl.

In another mixing bowl, beat the egg whites with the salt until they are foamy. Add the cream of tartar and beat until the whites hold a soft peak. Add the sugar, a little at a time, and continue beating until the egg whites are stiff but not dry. Beat in the vanilla extract.

Stir ¼ cup (60 grams) of the egg whites into the apricot mixture. Gently but quickly fold the remaining egg whites into the mixture.

Pour the batter into the prepared soufflé dish. Bake until the soufflé is risen and golden, about 25 to 30 minutes. Remove from the oven, remove the collar, and serve *immediately,* topped with whipped cream if desired.

serves 4 to 6

Fish

Fish and shellfish are cornerstones of the new cuisine. Perhaps more new entrées have been invented around sea creatures than any other category of foodstuffs. Nourishing, quick to prepare and low in fats, fish are a great source of culinary inspiration. Yet too often there are complaints: too many bones, smelly, dull, slimy. Too often these stem from bad buying and careless preparation.

Fish, more than anything else, suffers from careless handling at every stage of preparation. With the exception of skate (which needs a certain amount of aging) the dictum must be: the fresher the better! This is where you must trust your senses—after educating them, of course—to smell and look and feel. The fish must be firm, with a shiny, unblemished skin. Fresh fish has the delicate aroma of the sea; if it smells "fishy," it isn't fresh. Avoid frozen fish if at all possible.

One of the nicest things about fish is the vast variety, although the further inland you live, the less variety you can usually get. Which fish you choose is very much a function of how you wish to cook it. Delicate white fish such as trout demand gentle cooking and the least obtrusive of sauces and garnishes. More robust sea creatures—mackerel, swordfish, cod—can hold their own with powerful flavors. Some of the richer fish, however—salmon and tuna come to mind—are at their best simply grilled or poached.

In fact, the fresher the fish, the better it will be when served as simply as possible. The new cuisine has finally codified the notion that fish should be cooked for as short a time as possible. Otherwise, you will end up with rubbery or dry or disintegrated protein on the platter. The same is true for shellfish. Cook them gently…shrimps are done in under five minutes, molluscs as soon as they open their shells. Do not reheat most fish or shellfish, unless you are fond of the texture of old tires.

Most importantly, fish courses deserve careful presentation, gentle handling and piping hot plates. At their best, fish are as enticing as the azure seas from whence they come.

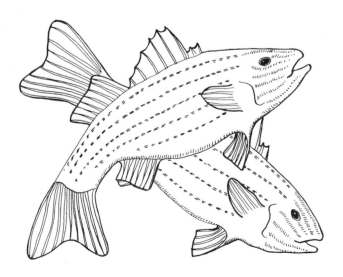

■ Poached Salmon with Rum Vinaigrette

1 6-pound (2.7 kg) cleaned fresh salmon
½ cup (4 fl oz or 120 ml) light rum
1¾ cups (14 fl oz or 420 ml) chicken broth
1 sliced onion
2 bay leaves
1 cup (225 grams) chopped celery leaves
1 lemon, thinly sliced
1 cucumber, thinly sliced
Rum Vinaigrette:
1½ cups (12 fl oz or 360 ml) olive oil
⅓ cup (3 fl oz or 80 ml) white wine vinegar
⅓ cup (3 fl oz or 80 ml) dark rum
1 teaspoon sugar
3 teaspoons salt
½ teaspoon freshly ground black pepper
1 teaspoon paprika
¼ cup (60 grams) chopped coriander
   (cilantro)
4 hard-cooked eggs, finely chopped

Preheat the oven to 375°F (190°C).

Put a large sheet of doubled heavy aluminum foil on a cookie sheet big enough to hold the salmon. Turn up the edges of the foil. Put the salmon on the sheet and add the rum, chicken broth, onion, bay leaves, celery leaves and lemon. Cover the salmon with another piece of foil and crimp the edges of the top and bottom sheets together to make a leakproof seam. Bake the salmon until it flakes easily, about 40 minutes.

Remove the salmon from the oven and let cool, still covered.

Put the olive oil, vinegar, dark rum, sugar, salt, pepper, paprika and coriander into the container of a food processor or blender. Process until thick.

Pour the vinaigrette into a mixing bowl and fold in the chopped eggs. Chill.

Remove the foil from the salmon. Pour off and discard the pan juices. Carefully strip the skin from both sides of the salmon and scrape off all dark meat. Cover with new foil and chill.

When ready to serve, remove the foil from the salmon and carefully transfer it to a large serving platter. Garnish with the lemon and cucumber slices. Stir the vinaigrette and pour some over each serving.
serves 6 to 8

■ Salmon with Lime and Walnut Oil

4 6- to 8-ounce (170 to 225 grams) fresh
   salmon fillets
salt to taste, if desired
freshly ground black pepper to taste
rind of 1 lime
7 tablespoons (100 grams) chilled sweet
   butter
2 tablespoons fresh lime juice
3 tablespoons walnut oil

Season the salmon fillets with salt and pepper.

Preheat the oven to 250°F (120°C).

Cut the lime rind into julienne strips. Blanch the strips in boiling water for 1 minute. Drain well.

Heat 2 tablespoons (30 grams) of the butter in a large skillet. Add the salmon fillets and sauté over medium-high heat until the fillets are lightly browned, about 4 minutes per side. Transfer the fillets to a plate, cover, and keep warm in the oven.

Add the lime juice, lime rind and walnut oil to the skillet. Stir well and cook over low heat until the mixture is just heated through. Whisk in the remaining butter 1 tablespoon (15 grams) at a time. Be careful not to let the sauce get too hot. Remove the skillet from the heat and let it cool slightly if necessary. The sauce should be slightly thick, about the consistency of hollandaise sauce. Season with salt and pepper and remove from the heat.

Remove the salmon fillets from the oven. Put one fillet on each of four individual serving plates. Spoon the sauce over the fillets and serve.
serves 4

■ Salmon with Scallops Filling and Lettuce Sauce

½ pound (225 grams) chilled fresh scallops
1 egg white
½ teaspoon fresh lemon juice
salt to taste, if desired
⅛ teaspoon cayenne pepper
⅛ teaspoon nutmeg
½ cup (4 fl oz or 120 ml) very well chilled
  heavy cream (single cream)
6 6- to 8-ounce (170 to 225 grams) fresh
  salmon fillets, about ½ inch thick (1.5 cm)
  thick
1 cup (8 fl oz or 240 ml) dry white wine
½ cup (4 fl oz or 120 ml) water
1 shallot, finely chopped
1 bay leaf
3 whole black peppercorns
¼ teaspoon dried tarragon
2 tablespoons (30 grams) sweet butter
1 head rinsed and dried Boston or any other
  soft lettuce
1 cup (8 fl oz or 240 ml) heavy cream (single
  cream)
freshly ground black pepper to taste

Put the scallops, egg white, lemon juice, salt, cayenne pepper and nutmeg into the container of a food processor or blender. Purée until smooth and well blended.

Pour the purée into a mixing bowl set into a larger mixing bowl filled with ice. Stir in the ½ cup (4 fl oz or 120 ml) of very well chilled cream, a little at a time. Stir well after each addition; do not add more cream until the previous addition is absorbed. Cover the mixture and refrigerate for 2 hours.

Trim the lettuce and cut it into julienne strips.

Spread the salmon fillets on a working surface. Spread the scallops mixture evenly over the fillets, leaving a 1-inch (2.5 cm) border all around. Starting at the narrow end of the fillet, roll the fillets up and fasten the rolls closed in place with wooden toothpicks.

In a skillet large enough to hold the salmon rolls in one layer, combine the wine, water, shallot, bay leaf, peppercorns and tarragon. Add the salmon rolls and cook over medium heat until the mixture just simmers. Cover the skillet and cook over very low heat until the filling is just set when tested with a fork, about 10 minutes.

While the salmon cooks, melt the butter in another skillet. Add the julienned lettuce, cover, and cook over low heat until just wilted, about 5 minutes. Stir occasionally. Put the lettuce into the container of a food processor or blender and process until smooth. Set aside.

Remove the salmon rolls from the skillet and put them on a plate. Set aside.

Strain the salmon cooking liquid through a fine sieve and return the liquid to the skillet. Discard any solids remaining in the sieve. Bring the liquid to a boil over medium heat. Continue to boil until the liquid is reduced to ¼ cup (2 fl oz or 60 ml). Add the cream and continue to boil until the sauce is thickened. Add the lettuce purée and stir well. Season with salt and pepper.

Slice the salmon rolls into ½-inch thick (2 cm) rounds. Remove the toothpicks. Distribute the sauce evenly among 6 individual serving plates. Put the salmon rounds on top of the sauce and serve immediately.

serves 6

■ Fresh Tuna in Lime and Ginger Marinade

½ cup fresh lime juice
2 garlic cloves, finely chopped
2 tablespoons olive oil
2 tablespoons vegetable oil
salt to taste, if desired
freshly ground black pepper to taste
1½ teaspoons finely chopped fresh ginger
1 teaspoon slivered lime rind
6 6- to 8-ounce (170 to 225 grams) fresh tuna steaks or John Dory, about 1 inch (2.5 cm) thick

Combine the lime juice, garlic, olive oil, vegetable oil, salt, pepper, ginger and lime rind in a mixing bowl. Whisk until well blended.

Put the tuna steaks into a shallow dish large enough to hold them in one layer. Pour the marinade over the fish. Turn the steaks to coat well. Cover the dish and marinate in the refrigerator for 4 hours, turning occasionally.

Preheat the broiler or prepare the cooker for grilling

Remove the tuna steaks from the marinade. Reserve the marinade. Grill the steaks 3 inches (8 cm) from the heat until lightly browned, about 3 to 5 minutes per side.

Put the reserved marinade into a saucepan and gently heat until hot.

Arrange the tuna on a serving platter and pour the hot marinade over each steak. Serve immediately.

serves 6

■ Red Snapper with Fresh Mint

1 3-pound (1.35 kg) cleaned whole red snapper, bass or halibut
salt to taste, if desired
freshly ground black pepper to taste
15 fresh mint sprigs
½ cup (4 fl oz or 120 ml) clarified butter

(see page 123)
3 tablespoons fresh lemon juice.

Preheat the oven to 400°F (200°C).

Season the cavity of the fish with salt and pepper. Stuff the cavity with 7 mint sprigs. Close the cavity with skewers or wooden toothpicks.

Rub the outside of the fish with ½ tablespoon of the butter and sprinkle with salt and pepper.

Put the fish on an oil baking sheet. Roast until the meat is just opaque near the bone, about 10 minutes per inch (2.5 cm) of thickness.

Prepare the sauce while the fish roasts. Chop the remaining mint. Heat the remaining clarified butter in a saucepan over low heat. Add the chopped mint and the lemon juice and stir well. Strain the sauce through a fine sieve and return it to the saucepan. Keep warm.

Remove the fish from the oven. Remove the skewers or toothpicks and fillet the fish. Lift the fillets from the fish, leaving the crisp skin intact, and put them on a serving platter. Pour the warm sauce over the fish and serve.

serves 4

■ Halibut Steaks with Red and Green Topping

2 teaspoons sweet butter
½ cup (120 grams) pecan halves
4 6- to 8-ounce (170 to 225 grams) halibut steaks, about 1 inch (2.5 cm) thick
salt to taste, if desired
freshly ground black pepper to taste
flour (plain flour) for dredging
4 tablespoons (60 grams) sweet butter
3 tablespoons vegetable oil
2 peeled celery stalks, cut into 1½ inch × ¼-inch (4 × 1 cm) strips
1 sweet red pepper, cut into 1½ × ¼-inch (4 × 1 cm) strips

Melt the 2 teaspoons butter in a skillet over moderately low heat. Add the pecans and the salt. Cook, stirring often, until the nuts are lightly toasted, about 2 minutes. Remove from the heat and set aside.

Season the halibut steaks on both sides with salt and pepper. Dredge the steaks in the flour and shake off any excess.

Melt the vegetable oil and 2 tablespoons (30 grams) of the butter in a large skillet over moderately high heat. Add the fish steaks and cook until lightly browned, about 4 minutes per side. Arrange the steaks on a serving platter large enough to hold them all in a single layer. Keep warm.

In another skillet, melt the remaining butter over low heat. Add the celery and red pepper strips and cook, stirring constantly, until tender, about 5 to 6 minutes.

Spoon the celery and red pepper over the halibut steaks. Sprinkle with the toasted pecans and serve at once.

serves 4

■ Red Snapper with Grapefruit

¼ *cup flour*
¼ *teaspoon paprika*
freshly ground black pepper
2 2-pound whole cleaned red snappers, bass
  or halibut with heads and tails
3 tablespoons vegetable oil
½ *cup sweet red pepper strips*
½ *cup green pepper strips*
1 carrot, peeled and cut into 1-inch rounds
1 onion, diced
2 garlic cloves, minced
1 tablespoon slivered ginger root
1 cup orange or pineapple juice
1 cup grapefruit segments, cut into 1-inch
  pieces
2 tablespoons wine or cider vinegar
1 teaspoon cornstarch (optional)

Combine the flour, paprika, and black pepper to taste in a large shallow dish. Dredge the fish on both sides in the mix-

ture. Shake off the excess.

Heat the oil in a large, heavy skillet over high heat. When the oil starts to bubble, add the fish and reduce the heat to medium. Brown each fish on both sides, about 5 minutes per side. Carefully remove the fish with two large spatulas and place them on a platter lined with paper towels.

Pour all but ½ teaspoon of oil from the skillet. Add the red pepper, green pepper, carrot, onion, garlic, and ginger. Add the fruit juice and mix well. Cover the skillet and simmer until the vegetables are tender but still crisp, about 12 to 15 minutes.

Add the grapefruit segments and vinegar to the skillet. Mix gently, then push the mixture to one side of the skillet. Return the fish to the skillet and cover. Cook until the fish flakes easily with a fork, about 5 minutes per side.

Remove the fish from the skillet and put it on a serving platter. If you prefer a thin sauce, simply spoon the grapefruit and vegetables over the fish and serve.

For a thicker sauce, remove ¼ cup of liquid from the skillet and put it into a small bowl. Add 1 teaspoon of cornstarch to the bowl and stir until dissolved. Pour the mixture back into the skillet and mix well. Cook over low heat until the sauce thickens, about 4 minutes. Pour the sauce over the fish and serve.

serves 4

■ Blackened Redfish

8 8- to 10-ounce (225 to 280 grams) skinned
  redfish or any other firm white fish fillets
2 cups (450 grams) sweet butter
¼ *cup (2 fl oz or 60 ml) fresh lemon juice*
1 tablespoon (15 grams) crumbled dried
  thyme
2 teaspoons freshly ground black pepper
1½ *teaspoons cayenne pepper*
1 teaspoon salt

Remove any small bones from the fish fillets, using a tweezers if necessary. Put the fillets into the refrigerator and leave until very well chilled. Do not remove the fillets until needed—they must be very cold.

In a large skillet, melt the butter over low heat. Add the lemon juice, thyme, pepper, cayenne pepper and salt. Stir well and cook for 10 minutes. Pour the mixture into a large, shallow dish and cool.

Heat a large, cast-iron skillet over high heat until it is very hot.

Remove the fish fillets from the refrigerator and dip them into the cooled butter mixture. In batches, put the fillets into the skillet. The fish will turn black and cook almost instantly. Turn and quickly cook on the other side. Remove the fillets from the skillet and keep warm on a plate. Cook the remaining fillets as above.

After all the fish has been cooked, add the remaining butter mixture to the skillet. Cook over high heat, stirring to loosen the brown bits on the sides and bottom of the skillet, until the butter is dark brown.

Spoon the browned butter over the fish and serve immediately.

serves 8

■ Striped Bass Baked with Fennel

1 4- to 5-pound (1.8 to 2.25 kg) cleaned
* whole striped or sea bass (rockfish)*
1 tablespoon walnut oil
2 teaspoons coarse salt
5 small fennel bulbs
2 large onions, thickly sliced
2 large tomatoes, thickly sliced and seeded
1½ cups (12 fl oz or 360 ml) dry white wine
* or dry vermouth*
2 cups (16 fl oz or 480 ml) heavy cream
* (single cream)*
4 tablespoons (60 grams) chilled sweet butter
2 tablespoons minced fennel fronds
salt to taste, if desired
lemon wedges for garnish
fennel fronds for garnish

Trim the tough outer ribs from the fennel bulbs and discard. Peel the bulbs, halve them lengthwise, and trim. Reserve the trimmings and the fronds. Set aside.

Preheat the oven to 400°F (200°C).

Gently pat the fish dry. Rub it inside and out with the walnut oil and sprinkle inside and out with the coarse salt. Measure the thickness of the fish to determine its cooking time later. Stuff the cavity of the fish with the reserved fennel trimmings.

Line a large roasting pan with a piece of aluminum foil folded in half lengthwise. Put the fish on the foil. Arrange the onion slices on top of the fish; arrange the tomato slices on top of the onion slices. Hold the slices in place with wooden toothpicks. Arrange the fennel bulbs around the fish and add the wine. Cover the pan securely with a piece of aluminum foil. Bake the fish for 9 minutes per inch (2.5 cm) of thickness, or until it is just opaque.

While the fish cooks, boil the cream in a saucepan until it is reduced to 1 cup (8 fl oz or 240 ml). Remove from the heat.

Remove the fish from the oven. Remove the toothpicks and the tomatoes and onions. Discard the onions. Chop the tomatoes finely and set aside. Reserve the pan juices.

Using the edges of the foil as handles, transfer the fish to a serving platter and keep warm. Arrange the fennel bulbs around the fish.

Strain the pan juices through a sieve into a saucepan. Discard any solids remaining in the sieve. Bring the pan juices to a boil and continue to boil until the sauce is reduced to about 1¾ cups (14 fl oz or 420 ml).

Remove the sauce from the heat and whisk in the butter, ½ tablespoon at a time. Add the minced fennel fronds and stir to blend. Season with salt if desired and pour the sauce into a sauceboat.

Arrange the chopped tomatoes, lemon wedges and fennel fronds around the fish. Serve with the sauce on the side.

serves 10

■ Sea Bass with Goat Cheese (*Chèvre*) Topping

2 tablespoons (30 grams) sweet butter, melted
4 6- to 8-ounce (170 to 225 grams) sea bass
    or red snapper fillets
coarse salt to taste, if desired
freshly ground black pepper to taste
⅓ cup (3 fl oz or 80 ml) dry vermouth
⅓ cup (3 fl oz or 80 ml) chicken broth
2 teaspoons fresh lemon juice
Goat Cheese Topping:
3 ounces (85 grams) Montrachet or other
    goat cheese, at room temperature
6 tablespoons heavy cream (single cream)
½ cup (120 grams) coarsely chopped walnuts
3 tablespoons sliced whole scallions (green
    onions)
2 tablespoons finely chopped fresh marjoram
    or 1 teaspoon dried
coarse salt to taste, if desired
freshly ground black pepper to taste

In a small bowl blend the softened goat cheese and the cream with a spoon until smooth. Add the walnuts, scallions (green onions), parsley, marjoram, salt and pepper. Blend well and set aside.

Preheat the oven to broil to prepare the cooker for grilling. Brush a broiling/grilling pan with 1 tablespoon of the melted butter.

Brush the fillets with the remaining butter. Season the fish on both sides with salt and pepper.

Grill the fillets 4 inches (10 cm) from the heat until the fish is not quite opaque in the center, about 9 to 10 minutes per inch (2.5 cm) of thickness.

Remove the pan and spread the topping evenly over the fish fillets. Return the pan and cook until the cheese begins to melt and the fish is opaque in the center, about 1 to 2 minutes longer. Remove the fillets from the pan and keep them warm on a plate.

Put the broiling/grilling pan over moderate heat and stir in the vermouth and chicken broth. Bring the mixture to a boil, stirring constantly to loosen the brown bits on the bottom of the pan. When the liquid comes to a boil, pour it into a small saucepan. Bring to the boil again. Continue to boil until the liquid is reduced to ⅓ cup (3 fl oz or 80 ml). Stir in the lemon juice and season to taste with salt.

Spoon the sauce over the fish and serve.

serves 4

■ Sautéed Sole with Hazelnuts

4 6- to 8-ounce (170 to 225 grams) skinned
    sole fillets
flour (plain flour) for dredging
3 tablespoons (45 grams) sweet butter
3 tablespoons olive oil
salt to taste, if desired
freshly ground black pepper to taste
4 thin lemon slices
⅔ cup (150 grams) raisins
⅓ cup (75 grams) halved hazelnuts
¼ cup (60 grams) pine nuts (pignoli)

Gently pat the sole fillets dry. Dredge the fillets in the flour, shaking off any excess.

In a large skillet heat the butter and oil together. When hot, add the fish fillets. Sauté until golden brown, about 2 to 3 minutes per side. Season with salt and pepper. Using a spatula, transfer the fish to a serving platter. Top each fillet with a lemon slice and keep warm.

Add the raisins, hazelnuts and pine nuts to the skillet. Sauté over low heat until the pine nuts are golden brown, about 5 minutes. Stir occasionally.

Spoon the sauce over the fish fillets and serve immediately.

serves 4

■ Cold Mussels in Spicy Sauce

5 pounds (2.25 kg) mussels, scrubbed,
    cleaned and debearded
¾ cup (6 fl oz or 180 ml) dry white wine
½ cup (4 fl oz or 120 ml) olive oil
2 onions, very finely chopped
4 garlic cloves, very finely chopped
2 teaspoons ground cumin
2 pounds (900 grams) ripe tomatoes, peeled,
    seeded and finely chopped
2 35-ounce (1 kg) tins Italian plum tomatoes,
    drained and finely chopped
4 4-inch (10 cm) hot green chili peppers,
    seeded and finely chopped
¼ cup (60 grams) finely chopped whole
    scallions (green onions)
¼ cup (60 grams) finely chopped fresh
    coriander leaves

Put the wine into a large heavy pot and add the mussels. Cover the pot and steam over high heat until the mussels open, about 5 to 8 minutes. Shake the pot occasionally. Discard any mussels that do not open.

Using a sloted spoon, transfer the mussels to a large, shallow baking dish. Reserve the liquid. Remove the top shells from the mussels and discard them. Release the mussels in the lower shells, but leave them in the shells. Loosely cover the dish with damp paper towels and plastic wrap. Refrigerate for 4 hours or overnight.

Strain the reserved cooking liquid into a bowl through a sieve lined with a double thickness of damp cheesecloth. Set aside.

Heat the olive oil in a skillet. When hot, add the onions and cook over moderate heat until softened, about 5 minutes. Add the garlic and cook, stirring constantly, until softened, about 2 to 3 minutes longer. Sprinkle the cumin over the onions and garlic and cook, stirring often, over low heat for 1 minute. Add the fresh and canned tomatoes and ¾ cup (6 fl oz or 180 ml) of the cooking liquid. Bring the mixture to a boil. Reduce the heat and simmer, stirring constantly, until the sauce has thickened slightly, about 10 minutes.

Add the chili peppers, scallions, salt and pepper. Stir well. Remove the skillet from the heat and let the sauce cool. Add the chopped coriander and stir well.

Remove the mussels from the refrigerator and arrange on four individual serving plates. Spoon the sauce into four individual small bowls and serve with the mussels for dipping.

serves 4

■ Creole Boiled Shrimp (Prawns)

100 shrimp (prawns) cleaned, shelled and
    deveined
3 tablespoons (45 grams) salt
1 large head celery, with leaves, coarsely
    chopped
1 teaspoon whole allspice
½ teaspoon mace slices
6 whole cloves
4 parsley sprigs
4 bay leaves
½ teaspoon dried thyme
1 dried hot red pepper
freshly ground black pepper to taste
cayenne pepper to taste

Fill a very large pot with water and add the salt, celery, allspice, mace, cloves, parsley, bay leaves, thyme, red pepper, black pepper and cayenne pepper. Bring the water to a boil. Continue to boil for 3 minutes.

Drop all the shrimp (prawns) into the pot. Boil until the shrimp (prawns) are bright pink, about 7 to 10 minutes. Remove the pot from the heat. Let the shrimp (prawns) cool in the pot. Serve at room temperature.

serves 8 to 10

■ John Clancy's Shrimp (Prawns) with Jalapeño Peppers

24 large shrimp (prawns), cleaned, shelled
  and deveined
cornstarch for dredging
salt to taste, if desired
⅓ cup (75 grams) sweet butter
2 tablespoons olive oil
⅓ cup (3 fl oz or 80 ml) dry sherry
4 canned jalapeño peppers, seeded and very
  thinly sliced

Season the shrimp (prawns) lightly with salt and dredge in the cornstarch. Roll the shrimp (prawns) to coat completely.

Put the shrimp (prawns) into a sieve and shake to remove excess cornstarch.

Melt the butter and oil together in a skillet over moderately high heat. Add the shrimp (prawns) and cook until just pink, about 3 to 4 minutes. Stir often.

Push the shrimp (prawns) to one side of the skillet. Add the sherry and jalapeño peppers to the other side and heat briefly. Carefully ignite the sherry, using a long match. Shake the skillet back and forth until the flame dies.

Transfer the shrimp (prawns) to a serving platter, pour the sauce over, and serve at once.

serves 4

■ Shrimp (Prawns) with Sun-Dried Tomatoes and Goat Cheese

¼ pound (120 grams) sun-dried tomatoes
  packed in olive oil
2 teaspoons finely chopped garlic
3 tablespoons rinsed and drained capers
½ teaspoon dried oregano
1½ pound (675 grams) large shrimp
  (prawns), cleaned, peeled and deveined
2 cups (450 grams) crumbled goat cheese

Preheat the oven to 450°F (230°C).

Chop the sun-dried tomatoes finely and reserve the olive oil. There should be about ½ cup (120 grams) of the tomatoes.

Put the tomatoes, reserved olive oil, garlic, 3 tablespoons olive oil, capers, oregano and shrimp (prawns) into a large mixing bowl. Mix well.

Fill four individual ramekins or 1¼ cup (10 fl oz or 300 ml) capacity individual soufflé dishes with the shrimp (prawns) mixture. Sprinkle the goat cheese evenly over each dish.

Bake until the cheese is melted, about 10 to 12 minutes. Serve immediately.

serves 4

■ Sautéed Crabs with Shallots and Prosciutto

5 tablespoons (75 grams) sweet butter
6 tablespoons finely chopped shallots
1 pound (450 grams) flaked and picked fresh
  crab meat
4 teaspoons finely chopped parsley
freshly ground black pepper to taste
16 thin slices prosciutto
1 lemon, very thinly sliced for garnish
watercress sprigs for garnish

Melt the butter in a skillet over moderately high heat. When the butter foams, add the shallots and sauté until softened, about 1 minute. Add the crab meat and sauté, stirring constantly, until heated through. Remove the skillet from the heat and stir in the parsley and black pepper.

Arrange 4 slices of prosciutto on each of four warmed individual serving plates. Top the prosciutto with equal portions of the crab mixture. Garnish with the lemon slices and watercress sprigs. Serve with more freshly ground black pepper.

serves 4

◼ Curried Shrimp (Prawns) and Scallops with Spinach

as served at the Washington Street Café, New York

½ cup (120 grams) sweet butter
4 tablespoons finely chopped onions
2 sweet red peppers, cut into rings
4 teaspoons finely chopped garlic
8 mushrooms, thinly sliced
4 tablespoons finely chopped whole scallion
  (green onion)
4 teaspoons curry powder
¼ teaspoon cayenne pepper
12 large shrimp (prawns), cleaned, shelled
  and deveined
12 large sea scallops
2 cups (16 fl oz or 480 ml) dry white wine
20 fresh spinach leaves, well rinsed
salt to taste, if desired
freshly ground black pepper to taste

Melt the butter in a skillet over medium-low heat. Add the onion, red peppers, and garlic. Cook, stirring constantly, until the onion is soft, about 5 minutes.

Add the mushrooms, scallions, curry powder, cayenne pepper, shrimp (prawns) and scallops. Stir until the shellfish are coated with the curry powder. Stir in the wine and cook over medium-high heat until the shrimp (prawns) and scallops are barely cooked, about 3 minutes. Add the spinach and cover the skillet. Cook until the spinach is wilted, about 1 minute. Season with salt and pepper, transfer to a serving platter, and serve at once.

serves 4

◼ Beer-steamed Mussels

5 pounds (2.25 kg) mussels, scrubbed,
  cleaned and debearded
1½ cups (12 fl oz or 360 ml) beer (lager)
2 garlic cloves, crushed
¼ teaspoon ground allspice
½ teaspoon hot red pepper flakes
½ bay leaf
2 parsley sprigs
½ cup (120 grams) sweet butter
2 tablespoons fresh lemon juice
1 teaspoon Dijon-style mustard
1 tablespoon finely chopped parsley
salt to taste, if desired
freshly ground black pepper to taste

Put the beer, garlic, allspice, red pepper flakes, bay leaf and parsley sprigs into a large pot. Add the mussels, cover, and steam over high heat until the shells open, about 5 to 8 minutes. Shake the pot occasionally. Discard any mussels that do not open.

Melt the butter with the garlic in a saucepan over medium heat. Add the lemon juice, soy sauce, mustard, chopped parsley, salt and pepper. Whisk to blend well. Cook until the sauce is hot. Remove the saucepan from the heat and discard the garlic cloves. Pour the sauce into a serving bowl. Distribute the mussels among four individual serving bowls and serve with the sauce.

serves 4

Poultry

According to the latest statistics, chicken may soon outrank beef as the favorite meat. And there are certainly good reasons for this expansion in popularity. Chicken is comparatively cheap, though free-range birds do cost quite a bit more. It is low in fat, comparatively high in nutrients and lends itself to perhaps more preparations than any other single protein source. It can be made to taste of almost anything, depending upon what is cooked with it. From the peppers and tomatoes and garlic of the Mediterranean to the warming brown fricassees of Burgundy and the middle European countries to the countless preparations of Italian cuisine, you can use the chicken as a canvas for flights of fancy.

Chicken has the advantage of being purchasable in parts. Thus, you can buy what your family prefers. Other poultry must be bought whole, but even so, ducks, turkeys, geese, pigeons, game hens and the entire gamut of game birds can but further widen you choices for creative good cooking. Remember, they need not be roasted. Some birds, especially the drier ones such as turkey and game, can benefit from longer, moist cooking methods, such as braising or stewing. Duck is a favorite of the new cuisine. In France the magrets—the breasts—from specially raised birds can be bought detached and trimmed. We don't have that luxury yet, but the breasts can be detached, either by the butcher or at home and the rest of the duck used for stock, reserving the legs to grill or for rillettes.

Turkey can be used instead of veal in many recipes, and has the advantage of being available as just the breast which is totally devoid of waste. Game, if you have access to it, adds variety and a touch of the exotic and elegant to the table. However, with few exceptions it is expensive to purchase and invariably tastes best when prepared in the simplest possible manner.

Whatever poultry you choose to cook, don't overcook it. Poultry is the most delicate protein food after fish and deserves constant attention on the stove or in the oven. Otherwise you will end up with a dry, dull dish.

◼ Roast Chicken

1 2½- to 3-pound (1.125 to 1.35 kg) chicken
4 tablespoons (60 grams) sweet butter,
 softened
salt to taste, if desired
freshly ground black pepper to taste
½ teaspoon dried chervil
½ cup (4 fl oz or 120 ml) or more warm
 chicken broth
3 tablespoons crème fraîche (see page 123)

Preheat the oven to 400°F (200°C).

Put the softened butter into a small mixing bowl. Mash the salt, pepper and chervil into the butter until well blended.

Clean, rinse and gently dry the chicken.

Put half the butter mixture into the chicken's cavity. Rub the remaining butter mixture over the outside of the chicken.

Put the chicken on its side on a rack in a roasting pan. Roast, basting with the pan juices every 25 minutes or so, until the juices run clear when the thigh is pricked with a fork, about 1 hour to 1 hour 15 minutes. Turn the chicken halfway through the roasting time.

Remove the chicken from the oven. Transfer it to a plate and keep warm. Pour off the fat from the roasting pan and add the chicken broth. Stir, scraping the brown bits from the sides and bottom of the pan. Set aside.

Remove and discard the skin from the breasts and thighs of the chicken. Slice the breasts and thighs, leaving the wings and drumsticks intact. Arrange the chicken on a platter.

Heat the chicken broth in the roasting pan. Season to taste with salt and pepper. Add the crème fraîche and stir well. Cook until the sauce is hot, but do not let it boil. Serve the chicken with the sauce in a sauceboat on the side.

serves 4

◼ Grilled Chicken with Mustard

1 2½- to 3-pound (1.125 to 1.35 kg) chicken,
 halved
salt to taste, if desired
freshly ground black pepper to taste
3 tablespoons Dijon-style mustard
2 tablespoons olive oil
1 tablespoon raspberry vinegar
2 tablespoons chopped watercress

Clean, rinse and gently dry the chicken halves.

Preheat the oven to broil or prepare the cooker for grilling.

Season the chicken halves with salt and pepper. Put the halves on a dish and brush generously on all sides with the mustard.

Put the chicken halves, skin-side up, into a baking dish large enough to hold them in one layer. Drizzle the olive oil over the chicken. Grill the chicken for 10 minutes. Turn the halves and grill for 10 minutes longer. Remove the dish from the broiler or cooker and pour off the fat. Turn the pieces skin-side up.

Set the oven to 400°F (200°C). Put the chicken into the oven and roast for 10 minutes.

Remove the chicken from the oven and put the dish on the stove over high heat. Add the vinegar to the dish and cook for 2 to 3 seconds. Remove the chicken pieces to a serving platter and cut into serving pieces. Pour the sauce over the chicken. Garnish with the chopped watercress and serve.

serves 4

Lemon with Rice Capers

Pasta with Uncooked Tomato Sauce (overleaf)

Green Noodles with Broccoli (page 56)

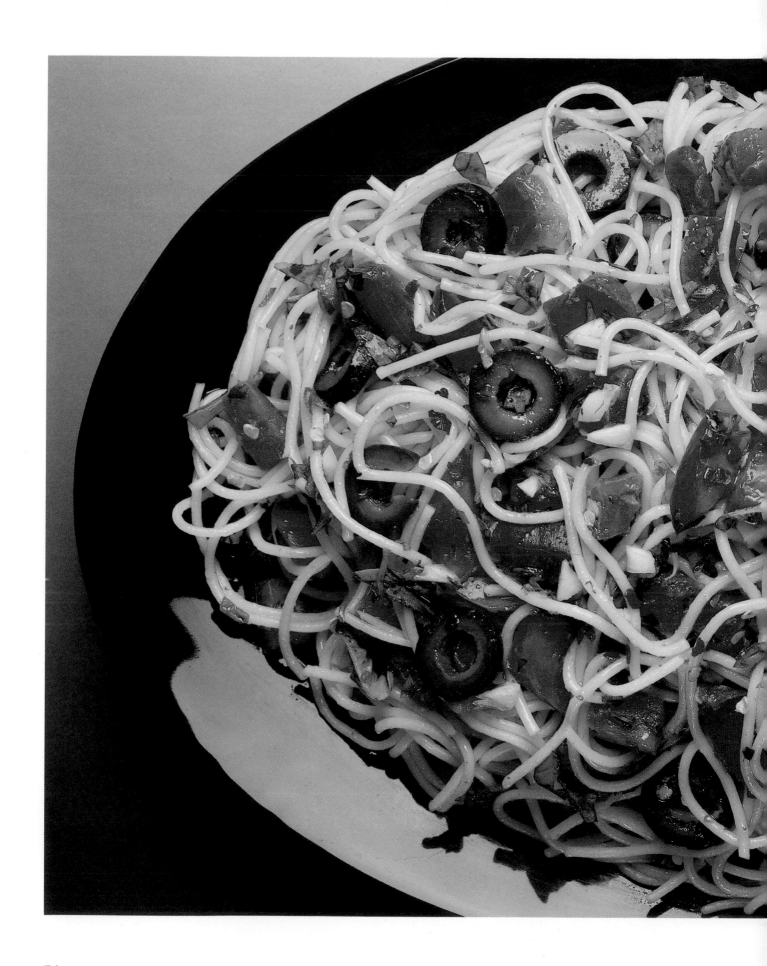

■ George Lang's Chicken Stuffed with Pasta

1 2½- to 3-pound (1.125 to 1.35 kg) chicken
olive oil
1 ounce (30 grams) dried mushrooms
¼ cup (2 fl oz or 60 ml) boiling water
2½ tablespoons (40 grams) sweet butter
2 chicken livers
¼ teaspoon dried thyme
¼ teaspoon cayenne pepper
2 ounces (60 grams) julienned fresh
  mushrooms
1 sweet red pepper, julienned
2 ounces finely chopped baked ham
2 tablespoons finely chopped parsley
2 ounces (60 grams) uncooked fettucini
salt to taste, if desired
freshly ground black pepper to taste

Clean, rinse and gently dry the chicken.

Put the dried mushrooms in a small bowl and pour the boiling water over them. Soak until the mushrooms are soft, about 15 minutes. Drain well. Rinse the mushrooms in cold water and drain well again. Cut off and discard the tough stems; chop the caps. Set aside.

Melt 1 tablespoon of the butter in a skillet over moderate heat. Add the chicken livers, thyme and cayenne pepper. Sauté until the livers are brown outside but still pink inside, about 5 minutes. Remove the livers from the skillet and chop them coarsely. Put the chopped livers into a mixing bowl.

Melt the remaining butter in the skillet. Add the fresh mushrooms and the sweet red pepper. Sauté over moderate heat until the liquid from the mushrooms has evaporated. Add the mushrooms and peppers to the mixing bowl with the chopped livers. Add the dried mushrooms, baked ham and chopped parsley to the mixing bowl. Mix well.

Cook the fettucini in boiling water until it is *al dente*. Drain well. Add the fettucini to the mixing bowl and toss well. Season to taste with salt and pepper.

Preheat the oven to 400°F (200°C).

Season the chicken inside and out with salt and pepper. Stuff the cavity of the chicken with the fettucini mixture, packing in as much as possible without compressing it. (Bake any extra stuffing in a covered baking dish for 20 to 25 minutes.) Tightly truss the chicken, being sure to close the cavity.

Put the chicken into a roasting pan. Brush the outside lightly with olive oil. Roast the chicken until the juices run clear when the thigh is pierced with a fork, about 50 minutes. Baste occasionally with the pan juices.

Remove the chicken from the oven and let stand for 5 minutes. Using poultry shears, cut the chicken into quarters. Arrange each portion on an individual serving plate, stuffing-side up. Serve at once.

serves 4

■ Chicken Breasts in Ginger Sauce

as served by Derek Hastings

4 whole chicken breasts, skinned, boned and
  halved
salt to taste, if desired
freshly ground black pepper to taste
flour (plain flour) for dredging
2 tablespoons (30 grams) sweet butter
2 tablespoons olive oil
2 finely chopped shallots
2 whole scallions (green onions), thinly sliced
2½ tablespoons (45 grams) finely chopped
  fresh ginger
½ cup (4 fl oz or 120 ml) dry white wine

Put each halved chicken breast between two sheets of waxed paper. With a meat mallet or the flat side of a heavy knife or cleaver, gently pound the chicken until it is ¼-inch (1 cm) thick. Season each piece with salt and pepper and dredge lightly in the flour. Shake off any excess.

Melt the butter and olive oil together in a skillet over medium heat. Add the chicken breasts and sauté until they are lightly browned, about 2 to 3 minutes per side. Remove the chicken from the skillet and keep warm on a serving platter.

Add the shallots and scallions (green onions) to the skillet. Sauté until softened, about 5 minutes. Add the ginger and white wine to the skillet and simmer, stirring constantly, for 2 to 3 minutes.

Spoon the sauce over the chicken breasts and serve.

serves 4

■ Chicken Sautéed with Lemon and Herbs

2 tablespoons finely chopped lemon rind
½ cup (4 fl oz or 120 ml) fresh lemon juice
4 tablespoons olive oil
½ cup (4 fl oz or 120 ml) dry white wine
1 teaspoon honey
salt to taste, if desired
freshly ground black pepper to taste
¼ cup (60 grams) finely chopped fresh
  rosemary, thyme and oregano, combined or
  1½ teaspoons each dried rosemary, thyme
  and oregano
4 large whole chicken breasts, skinned, boned
  and halved
2 tablespoons (30 grams) sweet butter
6 tablespoons heavy cream (single cream)
watercress sprigs for garnish
thin lemon slices for garnish

In a small bowl combine the lemon rind, lemon juice, 2 tablespoons olive oil, white wine, honey, salt, pepper, rosemary, thyme and oregano. Mix well.

Put the chicken pieces into a large shallow dish. Pour the marinade over the pieces and turn to coat well. Cover and refrigerate for 4 to 6 hours, turning occasionally.

Remove the chicken pieces from the marinade and gently pat dry.

Melt the butter and remaining olive oil together in a large skillet over medium-high heat. Add the chicken pieces and sauté until golden brown, about 5 to 7 minutes per side. Remove the pieces from the skillet and keep warm on a plate.

Pour off the liquid from the skillet. Add the reserved marinade and bring the mixture to a boil. Continue to boil until the marinade is reduced to ½ cup (4 fl oz or 120 ml). Stir in the cream and boil for 3 minutes longer.

Return the chicken pieces to the skillet. Cook until the chicken is heated through. Serve the chicken on a platter with the sauce poured over the pieces. Garnish with watercress and lemon slices and serve at once.

serves 4 to 6

■ Chicken Breasts Topped with Mustard

as served at The Bridge Café, New York

4 large whole chicken breasts
salt to taste, if desired
freshly ground black pepper to taste
4 tablespoons (60 grams) sweet butter, melted
½ cup (120 grams) Dijon-style mustard
½ cup (120 grams) grainy mustard
2 tablespoons fresh breadcrumbs
watercress sprigs for garnish

Insert the tip of a sharp boning knife under the tapered end of the breastbone of each breast. Remove the breastbone cartilage, leaving the ribs intact. Separate the breastbone from the flesh on both sides, being careful not to tear the skin. Grasp the tapered end of the breastbone and pull it up and away. Trim the breasts of excess fat and and pat dry.

Preheat the oven to broil or prepare the cooker for grilling.

Put the chicken breasts, skin-side up, into a broiling or grilling pan. Sprinkle with salt and pepper and drizzle with half the melted butter. Grill until the skin begins to be brown and crisp, about 5 minutes.

In a small bowl combine both mustards. Brush the skin side of the chicken breasts generously with the mixture. Drizzle the remaining butter over the breasts and sprinkle evenly with the breadcrumbs. Continue to grill until the chicken becomes slightly darker, about 2 to 3 minutes longer.

Set the oven to 400°F (200°C). Bake the chicken until it is firm and tender, about 6 to 12 minutes, depending on the size of the breasts.

Put the chicken pieces on a serving plate, garnish with watercress, and serve.

serves 4

■ Chicken Breasts Stuffed with Seasoned Goat Cheese (*Chèvre*)

3 ounces (85 grams) goat cheese
1 tablespoon thinly sliced whole scallion
  (green onion)
1 tablespoon chopped fresh mint
1 tablespoon fresh lemon juice
¾ teaspoon grated lemon rind
4 chicken breast halves, skinned and boned
4 teaspoons sweet butter
boiling water

Remove the rind from the cheese, if necessary, and bring to room temperature.

In a mixing bowl combine the cheese, scallion (green onion), mint, lemon juice and lemon rind. Mix with a fork until well blended.

Using a small, sharp knife, trim away any white tendons and excess fat from the chicken breasts. Carefully make a horizontal slit in the thickest part of each breast in order to form a small pocket. Be careful not to cut all the way through.

Gently stuff the cheese mixture into the pockets. Leave a ½-inch (1.5 cm) border at

the edge of each pocket. Press the edges of the pocket together to make a firm seal.

Cut four 10-inch (25 cm) squares from a sheet of heat-resistant plastic wrap. Put each breast half into the center of a square and top with 1 teaspoon (5 grams) of the butter. Wrap the breasts securely in the plastic and twist the ends to seal.

Put the wrapped breasts into a skillet large enough to hold them all snugly. Add enough boiling water to cover the breasts. Cover the skillet and poach over low heat until the centers of the chicken are opaque, about 8 minutes.

Remove the wrapped breasts from the skillet and carefully unwrap them. Cut each breast diagonally into four slices and arrange it on an individual serving plate. Serve immediately.

serves 4

■ Grilled Chicken with Artichoke and Lime Sauce

4 cucumbers
8 small or 4 large fresh artichokes
1 cup (8 fl oz or 240 ml) chicken broth
2 cups (16 fl oz or 480 ml) heavy cream
  (single cream)
¼ cup (2 fl oz or 60 ml) fresh lime juice
2 tablespoons (30 grams) sweet butter
4 whole chicken breasts, skinned and boned
¼ cup (2 fl oz or 60 ml) olive oil
1 tablespoon sesame oil
1 tablespoon tarragon vinegar

Peel and seed the cucumbers. Cut them into 1½-inch (4 cm) pieces. Cut each piece into very thin lengthwise strips. Put the strips into a bowl and add enough ice water to cover. Cover and refrigerate overnight.

Trim the artichokes and cook them in a steamer over boiling water until tender, about 40 minutes. Remove the artichokes from the steamer and let cool. When cool enough to handle, remove the leaves from the artichokes, reserving some for garnish. Discard the rest of the leaves and the chokes. Quarter the bottoms.

Bring the chicken broth to a boil in a saucepan over medium-high heat. Continue to boil until the broth is reduced to ½ cup (4 fl oz or 120 ml). Stir in the cream and continue to cook until the sauce is somewhat reduced and is thick enough to coat a spoon.

Pour the sauce into the container of a food processor or blender. Add the artichoke bottoms, lime juice, butter, salt and pepper. Process until the mixture is smooth. Pour the mixture into a saucepan and cover the top of the sauce with a piece of buttered waxed paper. Keep warm.

Put the chicken breasts between two pieces of waxed paper. Lightly pound with a meat mallet or the flat side of a heavy knife or cleaver until the breasts are flattened. Pat the breasts dry and season with salt and pepper.

Heat a grilling pan or ridged skillet over high heat until very hot. Brush the pan with 2 tablespoons of the olive oil and add two of the chicken breasts, skinned-side down. Sear for 1 minute. Give each breast a quarter turn and sear for 1 minute. Turn the breasts skinned-side up and sear for 1 minute. Remove the chicken from the pan and keep warm on a plate. Cook the remaining chicken breasts as above.

Drain the cucumbers well and put them into a skillet. Cook over medium-high heat, stirring constantly, until the cucumbers are just hot. Drain the cucumber well, pressing with the back of a spoon to remove as much liquid as possible. Put the cucumbers into a bowl and add the sesame oil, vinegar, salt and pepper. Toss well.

Divide the warm reserved sauce evenly among four heated individual serving plates. Coat the bottoms of the plates evenly. Put a mound of cucumbers into the center of each plate and top with a chicken breast. Garnish with the reserved artichoke leaves and serve.

serves 4

■ Chicken Livers in Wine

2 pounds (900 grams) fresh chicken livers
3 cups (24 fl oz or 720 ml) marsala or port
  wine
1 cup chopped whole scallions (green onions)
8 ounces (225 grams) sweet butter
flour (plain flour) for dredging
2 tablespoons fresh lemon juice
1 teaspoon dried sage
salt to taste, if desired
freshly ground black pepper to taste

Put the chicken livers in a bowl and cover with 2 cups (16 fl oz or 480 ml) of the marsala or port wine. Marinate for 1 hour.

Remove the livers from the wine and gently pat dry. Dredge very lightly in the flour, shaking off any excess.

Melt the butter in a skillet over medium-high heat. Add the chopped scallions (green onions) and sauté until softened, about 3 to 5 minutes. Add the livers to the skillet and sauté until they begin to stiffen, about 3 minutes. Add the remaining marsala or port wine, lemon juice, salt and pepper. Continue to cook the mixture over medium heat for 6 to 8 minutes, stirring occasionally.

Remove the livers from the skillet to a serving dish. Serve with the sauce poured over.

serves 4

■ Chicken Livers with Green Peppercorns

½ pound (240 grams) slab bacon (back bacon), thinly sliced
4 tablespoons (60 grams) sweet butter
4 tablespoons olive oil
2 pounds (900 grams) fresh chicken livers
4 shallots, finely chopped
1½ pounds (700 grams) fresh mushrooms, thinly sliced
⅔ cup (5 fl oz or 160 ml) dry sherry
1½ cups (12 fl oz or 360 ml) chicken broth
⅔ cup (5 fl oz or 160 ml) heavy cream (single cream)
1 teaspoon drained and rinsed green peppercorns
salt to taste, if desired
freshly ground black pepper to taste

Fry the bacon in a skillet over moderate heat until brown and crisp. Drain well on paper towels. Crumble the bacon and set aside.

Pour off the drippings from the skillet. Heat together 2 tablespoons (30 grams) of the butter and 2 tablespoons of the olive oil. When very hot, add the livers and sauté over very high heat, turning often, until they are browned on the outside and still pink on the inside, about 2 to 3 minutes. Remove the livers from the skillet and keep warm on a plate.

Add the remaining butter and olive oil

to the skillet and heat. Add the shallots and sauté, stirring often, until soft, about 2 to 3 minutes. Add the mushrooms and cook for 2 minutes longer. Remove the shallots and mushrooms from the skillet and add to the livers. Pour off the liquid in the skillet.

Add the sherry and chicken broth to the skillet. Bring the mixture to a boil over medium heat, stirring to loosen the brown bits on the sides and bottom of the skillet. Continue to boil until the liquid is reduced to 1 cup (8 fl oz or 240 ml). Stir in the cream and green peppercorns. Lower the heat and simmer until the sauce is slightly thickened. Do not boil. Season to taste with salt and pepper.

Return the chicken livers, bacon, mushrooms and shallots to the skillet. Cook until the livers are heated through. Transfer to a serving platter and serve at once.

serves 4

■ Grilled Duck with Black Currant Sauce

1 4½-pound (2 kg) duck, with neck removed
3½ cups (28 fl oz or 840 ml) dry red wine
½ cup (4 fl oz or 120 ml) black currant syrup or crème de cassis
2 bay leaves
1 onion, thinly sliced
1 carrot, thinly sliced
6 whole black peppercorns
1 teaspoon whole cloves
salt to taste, if desired
freshly ground black pepper to taste
1 cup (8 fl oz or 120 ml) chicken broth
¼ cup (60 grams) black currants
2 tablespoons (30 grams) sweet butter

Using a sharp knife or poultry shears, cut the wing tips from the duck, Split the duck. Clean and rinse the duck and gently pat it dry.

In a large bowl combine the wine, black currant syrup, bay leaves, onion, carrot, peppercorns and cloves. Mix well. Add the duck halves to the marinade. Turn to coat evenly. Cover the bowl and refrigerate for 6 hours or overnight, turning the duck occasionally.

Preheat the oven to 475°F (240°C) and prepare the coals for grilling.

Remove the duck halves from the marinade and pat dry. Reserve the marinade. Prick the skin of the duck all over with a fork, being careful not to pierce the meat.

Sprinkle the duck halves with salt and pepper to taste. Put them onto a roasting rack in a roasting pan and place in the oven for 20 minutes.

Strain the reserved marinade through a sieve into a saucepan. Discard any solids that remain in the sieve. Quickly bring the marinade to a boil. Continue to boil until it is reduced to ½ cup (4 fl oz or 120 ml), about 15 minutes. Skim the marinade if necessary and set aside.

Put the currants into a small bowl and add enough warm water to cover. Soak the currants until they are plump, about 10 minutes. Drain well.

Remove the duck halves from the oven and transfer them to a grill above the coals. Grill the halves, breast-side down, 3 inches from the coals for 25 to 30 minutes. Turn the halves and grill for 5 minutes longer.

Prepare the sauce as the duck grills. Add the chicken broth to the reduced marinade in the saucepan. Bring the mixture to a boil. Continue to boil until it is reduced to 1 cup (8 fl oz or 240 ml). Season with salt and pepper to taste and add the currants. Stir well. Whisk in the butter until it is well combined.

Remove the duck halves from the grill and put them onto a serving platter. Cut each half into half again and slice the breast meat. Serve the sauce in a sauceboat with the duck.

serves 2 to 4

■ Duck Breasts with Green Peppercorn Sauce

as adapted from Michel Guerard

6 duck breasts
1 cup (8 fl oz or 240 ml) white wine
⅓ cup (3 fl oz or 80 ml) cognac or brandy
1 to 3 tablespoons liquid from water-packed green peppercorns
½ cup (4 fl oz or 120 ml) chicken broth
1½ cups (12 fl oz or 360 ml) crème frâiche (see page 123)
salt to taste, if desired
1 tablespoon red wine vinegar
2 tablespoons port wine
2 tablespoons drained green peppercorns
3 teaspoons finely chopped roasted sweet red pepper

Put the wine and cognac into a saucepan and bring the mixture to a boil. Continue to boil until the mixture is reduced by two-thirds, about 5 to 7 minutes. Add the liquid from the green peppercorns and the chicken broth. Continue to boil for 5 minutes longer.

Add the crème frâiche and the salt. Cook at a gentle boil, stirring constantly, until the sauce is reduced by one-third, about 15 minutes.

In another saucepan, combine the vinegar and port. Cook over high heat until the liquid becomes syrupy and dark, about 30 seconds. Add the mixture to the crème frâiche mixture. Add the green peppercorns and the sweet red pepper. Stir well. Remove the saucepan from the heat and let cool.

Preheat the oven to broil or prepare the cooker for grilling.

Put the duck breasts on a rack in a broiling pan. Grill for 3 to 5 minutes on each side for medium-rare meat and longer for more well-done meat.

Return the sauce to the heat and cook just until it is heated through. Serve the breasts with the sauce in a sauceboat.

serves 6

Duck Poire William

2 5- to 6-pound (2.25 to 2.7 kg) ducks, necks removed
4 ripe pears, cored and very thinly sliced
⅔ cup (5 fl oz or 160 ml) pear liqueur
2 tablespoons olive oil
1 large piece fresh ginger, peeled
8 ounce (225 grams) drained straw mushrooms
8 ounces (225 grams) snow pea pods
2 cups (450 grams) thinly sliced scallions (green onions), green parts only
2 tablespoons sesame oil
salt to taste, if desired
freshly ground black pepper to taste

Preheat the oven to 325°F (170°C).

With a poultry shears or sharp knife, remove the wing tips from the ducks. Clean and rinse the ducks and gently pat them dry. Place the ducks, breast-side up, on a rack in a large roasting pan. Roast for 20 minutes.

After 20 minutes, prick the skin of the birds below the breast to release the fat. Continue to roast until the ducks are tender, about 1½ hours longer. Discard the fat from time to time.

In a bowl, pour the pear liqueur over the pear slices. Set aside.

Remove the ducks from the oven when they are done and let cool. Slice the meat and the skin from the ducks and reserve. Discard the carcasses.

Heat the olive oil in a large skillet. Add the ginger piece and cook until lightly browned, about 2 to 3 minutes. Add the duck pieces and cook, stirring constantly, for 3 minutes. Add the mushrooms and cook, stirring constantly, for 2 minutes. Add the snow peas and scallions and cook, stirring constantly, for 1 minute longer.

Add the pear slices and the liqueur. Cook, stirring constantly, until the pears are just soft, about 30 seconds. Season with sesame oil, salt and pepper. Discard the ginger piece and serve at once.

serves 6

Grilled Duck Breasts

as served at Caroline's, New York

8 duck breasts, skinned and boned
4 tablespoons (60 grams) whole black peppercorns
4 tablespoons (60 grams) very coarsely ground or crushed peppercorns
4 tablespoons (60 grams) chopped fresh thyme or 1½ teaspoons dried thyme
2 bay leaves
1 cup (8 fl oz or 240 ml) olive oil

Arrange the duck breasts in a shallow dish. Sprinkle them evenly with the whole peppercorns, crushed peppercorns, thyme and bay leaves. Pour the olive oil over the breasts. Cover the dish and refrigerate overnight.

Preheat the oven to broil or prepare the cooker for grilling.

Remove the duck breasts from the marinade and put them on a rack in a broiling pan. Grill the breasts for 3 to 5 minutes on each side for medium-rare meat and longer for more well-done meat. Serve the duck breasts with mild chutney or grainy mustard.

serves 4

Grilled Game Hens with Herbs

4 1- to 1½-pound (450 to 675 grams) Cornish game hens or pigeons
¼ cup (2 fl oz or 60 ml) fresh lemon juice
¼ cup (2 fl oz or 60 ml) olive oil
2 garlic cloves, finely chopped
1½ teaspoons chopped fresh thyme or ½ teaspoon dried thyme
½ bay leaf, crumbled
salt to taste, if desired
freshly ground black pepper to taste
4 large fresh rosemary sprigs or 1 teaspoon crumbled dried rosemary
4 tablespoons (60 grams) sweet butter, melted
fresh rosemary and watercress for garnish

Using a sharp knife, cut along one side of the backbone of each hen, from the neck to the tail. Spread the hens open and cut along the other side of the backbone, again from neck to tail. Remove the backbone. Put the hens on a cutting board, skin-side down. Pull out the breastbone and then flatten the hens with the side of a cleaver or large knife. Turn the hens over. Cut a slit across and through the skin between the lower breast and each thigh. Tuck the tips of the legs through the slits. Tuck the tips of the wings behind the shoulders. Remove any visible fat.

In a small bowl, combine the lemon juice, olive oil, garlic, thyme, bay leaf, salt and pepper.

Arrange the hens in two baking dishes. Place a sprig of fresh rosemary under each hen or sprinkle the undersides with dried rosemary. Divide the marinade evenly between the two baking dishes. Brush the hens with the marinade. Cover the dishes with aluminum foil and marinate the hens in the refrigerator for 4 hours or overnight, turning occasionally.

Preheat the oven to broil or prepare the cooker for grilling.

Remove the hens from the marinade and put them on a plate. Reserve the rosemary. Gently pat the hens dry.

Brush the hens with the melted buter and sprinkle them with salt and pepper. Top each hen with the reserved rosemary. Put the hens on a rack in a broiling pan, skin-side down, and cook 4 inches (10 cm) from the heat for 10 minutes. Turn and brush with the remaining butter. Grill until the juices run clear when the thigh is pierced with a fork, about 10 to 15 minutes longer.

Serve the hens on a large platter garnished with fresh rosemary and watercress sprigs.

serves 4

■ Nut-Stuffed Glazed Cornish Hens

6 1- to 1½-pound (450 to 675 grams)
  Cornish game hens or pigeons
6 tablespoons (90 grams) sweet butter
3 tablespoons finely chopped shallots
3 large mushrooms, finely chopped
4 cups (900 grams) cubed stale white bread
1 cucumber, peeled, seeded and finely
  chopped
½ cup (120 grams) coarsely chopped
  macadamia nuts or walnuts
½ cup (120 grams) golden raisins
1 teaspoon crumbled dried sage
salt to taste, if desired
freshly ground black pepper
⅓ cup (3 fl oz or 80 ml) dry white wine
¼ cup (60 grams) sugar
1 tablespoon white wine vinegar
¼ teaspoon cream of tartar
¾ cup (6 fl oz or 180 ml) fresh orange juice
rind of 1 orange, cut into thin strips
¼ cup (60 grams) mango chutney (see page
  122)
2 tablespoons (30 grams) sweet butter, melted

Heat the 6 tablespoons (90 grams) butter in a large skillet over medium heat. Add the shallots and cook, stirring constantly, until softened, about 5 minutes. Remove the skillet from the heat. Add the mushrooms, bread cubes, cucumber, macadamia nuts, raisins, sage, salt, pepper and wine. Mix the stuffing well and set aside.

Combine the sugar, vinegar and cream of tartar in a saucepan. Cook over medium heat, stirring often, until the mixture is pale brown. Remove the saucepan from the heat and add the orange juice and orange rind. Stir well and return the saucepan to the heat. Cook, stirring constantly, until smooth. Add the mango chutney and stir until the glaze is well blended. Remove the saucepan from the heat and set aside.

Preheat the oven to 400°F (200°C).

Pack the cavity of each hen loosely with

the stuffing. Truss the hens with white kitchen twine and sprinkle them with salt and pepper. Put the hens on a rack in a large roasting pan. Brush them with the melted butter and roast for 30 minutes. Lower the oven temperature to 350°F (180°C) and roast for 15 minutes longer.

Brush the hens with the glaze and continue to roast, basting every 10 minutes with the glaze, until the juices run clear when the thigh is pricked with a fork, about 30 minutes longer.

Remove the hens from the oven. Remove the twine, transfer to a platter, and serve.

serves 6

■ Quail Stuffed with Grapes

8 quails
juice of 2 lemons
salt to taste, if desired
freshly ground black pepper to taste
8 teaspoons (25 grams) sweet butter
2½ cups (550 grams) seedless red grapes
6 to 8 tablespoons (90 to 120 grams) sweet
  butter
1 cup (8 fl oz or 240 ml) white wine

Clean, wash, and dry the quails.

Sprinkle the quails with the lemon juice and season them with salt and pepper to taste.

Stuff the cavity of each bird with ¼ cup (110 grams) of the grapes and 1 teaspoon butter. Let the birds dry for 15 to 20 minutes.

Heat the 6 tablespoons (90 grams) butter in a heavy skillet. Add the quails and brown on all sides, turning often. Add more butter if needed. Add the white wine and cover the skillet. Simmer over moderate heat for 15 to 20 minutes.

Add the remaining grapes to the skillet and simmer for 5 minutes longer. Spoon the juices over the birds before serving.

serves 4

■ Squab or Pigeon with Crème Fraîche and Raspberry Vinegar

4 squabs or pigeons
3 tablespoons (1 fl oz or 45 ml) clarified
  butter (see page 123)
¾ cup (6 fl oz or 180 ml) raspberry vinegar
2 teaspoons finely chopped shallots
⅛ teaspoon crumbled dried tarragon
1 cup (8 fl oz or 240 ml) crème fraîche, at
  room temperature (see page 123)
salt to taste, if desired
freshly ground black pepper to taste
watercress sprigs, for garnish
fresh raspberries, for garnish

Rinse the squabs or pigeons and gently pat dry. Put each squab on a cutting board. With a sharp knife or poultry shears, cut along both sides of the backbone of each squab; remove the backbone. Put the squabs skin-side down. Using a sharp boning knife, cut the flesh away from the breastbone; remove the breastbone. Carefully cut the flesh away from the ribs. Cut each squab in half.

Preheat the oven to 400°F (200°C).

Heat the butter in a large skillet. When the butter is very hot, add the squabs, skin-side down. Sauté over moderate heat until the squabs are lightly browned, about 5 minutes per side.

Push the squabs to one side of the skillet. Spoon off all but a thin layer of butter and fat and add the vinegar, shallots and tarragon to the skillet. Bring the mixture to a boil and continue to boil for 5 minutes. Spoon some of the mixture over the squabs as they cook and turn the squabs once.

Remove the squabs from the skillet and put them into a baking dish. Roast, uncovered, for 15 minutes. Remove the squabs from the oven and transfer to a platter. Keep warm.

Bring the vinegar mixture in the skillet back to a boil. Cook, scraping the sides and bottom of the pan to loosen the brown bits, until the mixture is thick and syrupy, about 5 minutes. There should be about ¼ cup (2 fl oz or 60 ml).

Add the crème frâiche to the mixture in the skillet and stir. Bring the mixture to a boil over moderately high heat and cook until it is slightly thicker, about 5 minutes. Season to taste with salt and pepper.

Pour any juices from the baking pan into the crème frâiche mixture. Bring the mixture to a boil over moderately high heat and cook until the sauce has thickened slightly again, about 2 minutes.

Spoon the crème frâiche sauce into a large, deep serving platter. Put the squabs on top of the sauce. Garnish with watercress sprigs and fresh raspberries and serve at once.

serves 4

■ Turkey Scallops with Mushroom, Lemon and Caper Sauce

2 pounds (900 grams) thinly sliced fresh turkey breast
flour (plain flour) for dredging
2 tablespoons olive oil
6 tablespoons (90 grams) sweet butter
salt to taste, if desired
freshly ground black pepper to taste
½ pound (225 grams) fresh mushrooms, thinly sliced
½ cup (4 fl oz or 120 ml) dry white wine
¾ cup (6 fl oz or 180 ml) chicken broth
3 tablespoons fresh lemon juice
2 tablespoons chopped parsley
2 tablespoons rinsed and drained capers
2 lemons, sliced paper-thin

Put the turkey slices between two sheets of waxed paper and lightly pound them with a meat mallet or the side of a heavy knife or cleaver. Dredge the slices in the flour, shaking off any excess.

Melt 2 tablespoons (30 grams) of the butter and the olive oil together in a large skillet over moderately high heat. When very hot, add as many turkey slices as will fit comfortably. Sauté the slices until browned, about 1 to 2 minutes per side. Remove the slices from the skillet and keep warm on a plate. Season with salt and pepper. Cook the remaining turkey slices as above.

Melt 2 tablespoons (30 grams) of the butter in the skillet. Add the mushrooms and sauté, stirring constantly, for 3 to 4 minutes. Add the wine, chicken broth and lemon juice. Stir well and bring the mixture to a boil. Continue to boil until the sauce is slightly thickened, about 3 minutes. Add the remaining butter and whisk to blend. Add the chopped parsley and salt and pepper to taste. Stir well.

Return the turkey slices to the skillet and cook until they are heated through. Transfer the turkey to a serving platter and spoon the sauce over the slices. Sprinkle with the capers and top the turkey slices with the lemon slices. Serve immediately.

serves 6 to 8

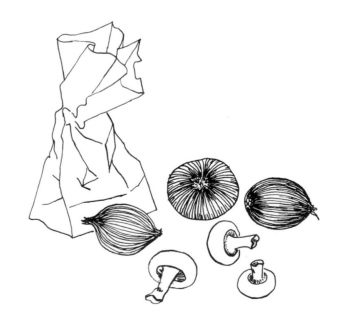

Meat

Man may be a carnivore, but evidence suggests that this is less and less the case. The new cuisine has, from the very beginning, taken notice of this by deemphasizing the massive portions of flesh that used to grace our plates. No hunks of steak or double-thick chops penetrate the new cuisine. More than likely instead you will find thin scallops or slices of veal or lamb cooked quickly and sauced moderately with natural juices and fresh herbs.

This is not merely a revulsion against largesse. Rather, the new cookery has taken into account contemporary life-styles. Shorter cooking times, simpler sauces, smaller portions all make for healthier eating, less weight gain and quicker preparation. However, quick-cooking meats must be of prime or choice quality. Few bargains can be found unless one wishes to explore the lesser-known cuts such as breast of veal, shanks, tails and necks. So long the province of the thrifty farm wife, these cuts demand the same care in buying and precision in cooking as any other comestible.

Beef, due to its heavy fat content, is less in favor than ever before. Pork, in fact, as raised today, is lower in saturated fats than beef and certainly fuller and more exciting in flavor. Rarely does pork appear with the flabby insipidity that sometimes comes with unaged beef. Veal and lamb, however, are the true favorites of the new cuisine, partially because they are the favorite meats in France where it all began, but also because they are meats more conducive to external influences. Veal in particular has the nice habit of taking on whatever flavors it is cooked with. Fresh herbs, wine, vegetables, good butter all enhance veal. Cream sauces do not.

When you serve meat or poultry, and in Anglo-Saxon countries it is certainly still the mainstay of every menu, don't overwhelm the diner with great slabs. Try a smaller portion, prepared with a bit more imagination and eclát. The difference will be appreciated.

■ Pork Tenderloin with Currant Sauce

1 cup (8 fl oz or 240 ml) chicken broth
⅓ cup (75 grams) packed currants or raisins
2 ¾- to 1-pound (350 to 450 grams) pork
* tenderloins*
6 ounces (180 grams) sweet butter
flour (plain flour) for dredging
½ cup (4 fl oz or 120 ml) sherry vinegar
salt to taste, if desired
freshly ground black pepper to taste

Put the chicken broth in a small saucepan and bring it to a boil. Put the currants into a small bowl and pour the hot broth over them. Soak until soft, about 30 minutes.

Beginning at the thicker end, slice each tenderloin into 6 ½-inch (1.5 cm) thick slices. Reserve the smaller ends of the tenderloins for another use.

Place each slice of pork between two sheets of waxed paper. Using a mallet or the flat side of a heavy cleaver or knife, pound each slice until it is a thin, 3-inch (8 cm) circle. Dredge the pork scallops in the flour and shake off any excess.

Melt 4 tablespoons (60 grams) of the butter in a skillet over medium heat. In batches, sauté the scallops until they are lightly browned, about 3 to 4 minutes each side. As the scallops are cooked, transfer them to a plate and keep warm.

When all the scallops have been cooked, add the vinegar to the skillet and quickly bring to a boil. Continue to boil, scraping the bottom and sides of the pan to loosen the brown bits, until the vinegar has a thick, syrupy consistency, about 5 minutes.

Add the currants and chicken broth to the skillet and bring to a boil. Reduce the heat. Return the pork scallops to the skillet and season with salt and pepper to taste. Cover and cook gently for 4 to 5 minutes.

Using a spatula or slotted spoon, transfer the pork to a serving platter. Reduce the heat to very low. Whisk the remaining butter, 1 tablespoon (15 grams) at a time, into the sauce in the skillet. After all the butter has been added, taste the sauce. Add 1 tablespoon additional vinegar if desired. Pour the sauce over the pork scallops and serve.

serves 4

■ Grilled Beef with Green Peppercorn Butter

1 cup (8 fl oz or 240 ml) dry red wine
½ cup (4 fl oz or 120 ml) olive oil
1 shallot, minced
1 teaspoon finely chopped fresh chives
3 garlic cloves, finely chopped
1 teaspoon salt, if desired
½ teaspoon whole black peppercorns
½ teaspoon dry mustard
½ teaspoon dried thyme
4 parsley sprigs
1 bay leaf
3 pounds (1.35 kg) top round (topside) steak,
* 2 inches (5 cm) thick*
1½ tablespoons crushed black peppercorns
½ cup (120 grams) Green Peppercorn Butter
* (see page 120)*

Combine the wine, olive oil, shallot, chives, garlic, salt, peppercorns, mustard, thyme, parsley and bay leaf in a large, shallow glass or ceramic (not metal) bowl. Stir well. Add the steak to the bowl and turn to coat evenly. Cover the bowl and marinate in the refrigerator for 4 hours or overnight, turning occasionally.

Remove the meat from the marinade and gently pat dry. Press the crushed black peppercorns into both sides of the steak. Allow the steak to stand at room temperature for 30 minutes.

Grill the steak over hot coals or in an oven or cooker. Cook for 8 to 10 minutes per side for rare meat; cook longer on both sides for more well done meat.

Put the steak on a cutting board. Brush the meat with half of the green peppercorn butter and let stand for 10 minutes. Thinly slice the meat diagonally against the grain. Dot the slices with the remaining butter and serve.

serves 6

■ Oriental Glazed Pork Ribs

as served at Chinois', Los Angeles, California

5 racks baby pork ribs, totaling 4 to 5 pounds
    (1.8 to 2.25 kg)
Marinade:
2 cups (1¼ pints or 720 ml) rice wine
    vinegar
1 cup (8 fl oz or 240 ml) soy sauce
1¼ cups (½ pint or 300 ml) honey
6 shallots, finely chopped
10 garlic cloves, finely chopped
2 tablespoons slivered fresh ginger
Sauce:
4 red onions, finely chopped
1 cup (8 fl oz or 240 ml) rice wine vinegar
6 tablespoons (3 fl oz or 80 ml) soy sauce
½ cup (4 fl oz or 120 ml) honey
1 cup (8 fl oz or 240 ml) chicken broth
¾ cup (6 fl oz or 180 ml) plum wine
3 tablespoons fresh lemon juice
2 shallots, finely chopped
½ cup (120 grams) chopped fresh coriander
    (cilantro)
½ cup (120 grams) chopped fresh parsley
1 pound (450 grams) sweet butter

In a container large enough to hold all the ribs, combine the rice vinegar, soy sauce, honey, shallots, garlic and ginger. Add the ribs and turn to coat. Cover the container and marinate in the refrigerator, turning occasionally, for 24 hours.

Set one of the oven racks in the middle of the oven; remove the others. Preheat the oven to 450°F (230°C).

In a large saucepan combine the onions, vinegar, soy sauce, honey, chicken broth, plum wine, lemon juice, shallots, coriander and parsley. Stir well and cook over high heat until the mixture is reduced to one-quarter the original amount, about 15 to 20 minutes.

Remove the saucepan from the heat. Whisk the butter, 1 tablespoon (15 grams) at a time, into the sauce.

In batches, put the sauce into the container of a food processor or blender and process until smooth. Return the sauce to the saucepan and reserve.

Remove the ribs from the refrigerator. Put the ribs on a rack in a roasting pan. Roast the ribs in the oven until glazed, about 35 minutes. Remove the ribs from the oven and place on a cutting board. Using a sharp knife, cut the rack apart into individual ribs.

The ribs may have to be roasted in batches if the oven is not a very large one. When ready to serve, warm all the ribs in the oven at 350°F (180°C) for 15 to 20 minutes. Reheat the sauce and serve it on the side with the ribs.

serves 8 to 10

■ Grilled Lamb with Kiwi

1 pound (450 grams) boneless leg of lamb
3 tablespoons olive oil
1 tablespoon fresh lemon juice
1 tablespoon soy sauce
freshly ground black pepper to taste
1 tablespoon light brown sugar
6 peeled kiwi fruits, cut into wedges

Trim the lamb of fat and cut it into 1-inch (2.5 cm) cubes.

Combine 1 tablespoon of the olive oil, the lemon juice, soy sauce and pepper in a shallow bowl. Add the lamb and mix well. Marinate the lamb at room temperature for 1 to 2 hours, stirring occasionally.

Combine the remaining olive oil and the brown sugar in a small bowl. Mix well.

Put alternate cubes of lamb and wedges of kiwi on skewers. Grill the kebabs over hot coals or in an oven or cooker, turning often, until done, about 8 minutes. Baste the kebabs with the brown sugar as they cook.

serves 4

■ Paul Prudhomme's Roasted Pork with Gingersnap Gravy

2 teaspoons freshly ground black pepper
1½ teaspoons salt, if desired
1 teaspoon white pepper
1 teaspoon cayenne pepper
1 teaspoon sweet paprika
1 teaspoon crumbled dried thyme
½ teaspoon dry mustard
3 tablespoons (45 grams) sweet butter
1 tablespoon vegetable oil
½ cup (120 grams) finely chopped onion
½ cup (120 grams) finely chopped celery
½ cup (120 grams) finely chopped green
  pepper
1 tablespoon finely chopped garlic
1 4-pound (1.8 kg) boneless pork loin
6 cups (2½ pints or 1.5 litre) chicken broth

Gingersnap Gravy:
1 teaspoon freshly ground black pepper
½ teaspoon salt, if desired
½ teaspoon white pepper
½ teaspoon ground ginger
½ teaspoon crumbled dried thyme
¼ teaspoon crumbled dried sage
¼ teaspoon cayenne pepper
⅛ teaspoon ground cumin
2 tablespoons (30 grams) sweet butter
2 tablespoons vegetable oil
¾ cup (180 grams) finely chopped onion
½ cup (120 grams) finely chopped celery
½ teaspoon finely chopped fresh ginger
8 gingersnap cookies, crumbled
1 tablespoon packed light brown sugar
1 teaspoon ground ginger

In a large skillet combine the black pepper, salt, white pepper, paprika, thyme and mustard. Add the butter, oil, chopped onion, celery, green pepper and garlic. Cook over high heat until the vegetables begin to soften, about 4 to 5 minutes. Remove the skillet from the heat and let cool completely.

Preheat the oven to 275°F (140°C).

Put the boneless pork loin in a roasting pan, fat-side up. Using a sharp knife, make 2 or 3 large slits in the roast. Spoon some of the cooled vegetable mixture into the slits. Rub the roast with the remaining vegetable mixture, spreading it generously over the top and sides. Roast the pork for 2½ hours, or until a meat thermometer inserted into the center of the roast reads 180°F (80°C). Raise the oven temperature to 425°F (220°C) and roast until the top of the pork is brown, about 8 minutes longer.

Remove the pork roast from the oven and put it on a serving platter. Pour the pan drippings into a measuring cup. Add enough chicken broth to make 1 cup (8 fl oz or 240 ml).

To make the gravy, in a small bowl combine the black pepper, salt, white pepper, ginger, thyme, sage, cayenne and cumin. Set aside.

In a large skillet, heat the butter and oil together over moderate heat. When the butter has almost all melted, add the chopped onion, celery and garlic. Cook, stirring occasionally, until the vegetables have softened, about 5 minutes. Stir in the reservered seasoning mixture and cook 5 minutes longer to blend the flavors.

Add the chicken broth and the pan drippings to the mixture in the skillet and quickly bring it to a boil. Continue to boil until the mixture is reduced to about 4 cups (1¾ pint or 1 litre), about 25 to 30 minutes.

Add the crumbled gingersnaps to the skillet and gently whisk until the crumbs are softened. Continue to cook, whisking constantly, until the crumbs have completely dissolved, about 10 minutes longer. Add the brown sugar and ground ginger. Stir well. Strain the gravy through a sieve, discarding the solids that remain.

Slice the pork roast and arrange the slices on a serving platter. Pour some of the gravy over the slices, and serve the rest in a sauceboat on the side.

serves 6

■ Glazed Baked Ham

1 8-pound (3.6 kg) precooked ham with bone
whole cloves
2 tablespoons Dijon-style mustard
¼ cup (60 grams) packed dark brown sugar
1 cup (8 fl oz or 240 ml) Madeira wine
½ cup (4 fl oz or 120 ml) apricot nectar
½ cup (4 fl oz or 120 ml) apple juice

Preheat the oven to 350°F (180°C).

Using a sharp knife, trim the skin from the ham. Trim off any excess fat, leaving a thin layer on the meat. Score the fat layer in a diamond pattern.

Put the ham in a shallow roasting pan. Spread the top and sides evenly with the mustard and stick a clove into the center of each diamond. Sprinkle the brown sugar evenly over the top of the ham.

Roast the ham for 10 minutes per pound (450 grams), about 1 hour and 20 minutes for an 8-pound (3.6 kg) ham.

Combine the Madeira, apricot nectar and apple juice in a small bowl. Mix well. Baste the ham with the mixture every 12 to 15 minutes as it roasts.

Remove the ham from the roasting pan and put it on a serving platter. Pour the pan drippings into a saucepan. Combine any remaining basting liquid with enough water to make 1 cup (8 fl oz or 240 ml). Add to the drippings. Quickly bring the mixture to a boil and cook for 1 to 2 minutes. Pour the sauce into a sauceboat and serve with the thinly sliced ham.

serves 10 to 12

■ Lamb with Fresh Herbs

¼ cup (2 fl oz or 60 ml) olive oil
4 lamb scallops or lamb chops (cutlets)
1 shallot, finely chopped
1 garlic clove, crushed
1 teaspoon finely chopped fresh basil or ¼
*   teaspoon crumbled dried basil*
1 teaspoon finely chopped fresh thyme or ¼
*   teaspoon crumbled dried thyme*
1 teaspoon finely chopped fresh tarragon or
*   ¼ teaspoon crumbled dried tarragon*
1 cup (8 fl oz or 240 ml) dry white wine or
*   dry vermouth*
2 tablespoons crème frâiche (see page 123)
3 tablespoons (45 grams) chilled sweet butter,
*   cut into 3 equal pieces*
salt to taste, if desired
freshly ground black pepper to taste
chopped fresh chives for garnish

Heat the olive oil in a large, heavy skillet over moderately high heat. When very hot, add the lamb. Sear the lamb on each side, about 3 to 4 minutes per side or longer for more well-done meat. Put the lamb on a plate and keep warm.

Pour off all but a thin layer of the olive oil from the skillet. Add the shallots and sauté until softened, about 3 minutes. Add the garlic and the herbs. Stir well and cook for 30 seconds. Add the wine and stir well, scraping the sides and bottom of the skillet to loosen all the brown bits. Quickly bring the mixture to a boil and continue to boil until the sauce is reduced by half. Add the crème frâiche and stir. Continue to boil until the sauce is thickened and reduced.

Lower the heat. Whisk in the butter, 1 tablespoon (15 grams) at a time. Continue to whisk until the sauce is well blended. Season with salt and black pepper to taste.

Spoon the sauce over the warm lamb. Garnish with the chopped chives and serve.

serves 4

■ Lamb Chops (Cutlets) with Vegetable Purée

4 cups (900 grams) fresh peas, shelled
boiling water
4 tablespoons heavy cream (single cream)
salt to taste, if desired
freshly ground black pepper to taste
3 tablespoons chopped fresh mint leaves
½ cup (120 grams) sweete butter, softened
8 small lamb chops (cutlets)
⅛ teaspoon sugar

Cook the peas in a saucepan of boiling water until tender, about 6 to 10 minutes. Drain well.

Put the peas into the container of a food processor or blender and process until a smooth purée is formed. Press the purée through a sieve into a saucepan. Discard any solids remaining in the sieve.

Add the cream to the purée by tablespoons, stirring well after each addition. Do not add all the cream if the purée seems too thin. Season with salt and pepper and gently cook the purée over low heat until it is heated through. Set aside.

In a small bowl combine the chopped mint leaves and butter. Season with salt and pepper, cover, and chill.

Preheat the oven to broil or prepare the cooker for grilling.

Generously season the lamb chops with salt and pepper. Grill the chops until they are done to taste, about 4 to 5 minutes per side.

As the lamb chops cook, reheat the pea purée over low heat until it is hot. Add half the mint butter to the purée and stir. Continue to cook only until the butter is absorbed. Remove the purée from the heat and stir in the sugar.

To serve, cover the bottom of each individual serving plate with a layer of the purée. Top each layer with 2 lamb chops. Top each chop with ½ teaspoon of the mint butter. Serve at once.

serves 4

■ Leg of Lamb with Cheese

1 7-pound (3 kg) leg of lamb, boned and
  butterflied
¼ cup (2 fl oz or 60 ml) olive oil
2 teaspoons finely chopped garlic
1 teaspoon crumbled dried tarragon
¼ cup (2 fl oz or 60 ml) Dijon-style mustard
½ cup (4 fl oz or 120 ml) freshly grated
  Parmesan cheese
3 tablespoons finely chopped parsley
2 tablespoons bread crumbs
2 tablespoons (30 grams) sweet butter, melted

Combine the olive oil, garlic and tarragon in a small bowl. Brush the mixture over the lamb and let the lamb stand for 2 to 3 hours at room temperature.

Preheat the oven to broil or prepare the cooker for grilling. Put the lamb, fat-side down, in a shallow roasting pan. Brush the top of the lamb with half the mustard and grill for 5 minutes. Turn the lamb over, brush with the remaining mustard and grill for 5 minutes longer. Remove the lamb from the heat.

Reduce the oven temperature to 450°F (230°C).

In a small bowl, combine the cheese, parsley and breadcrumbs. Sprinkle the mixture over the lamb, patting gently to make the crumbs stick. Drizzle the melted butter over the top. Put the lamb in the oven and roast until the meat is pink and the crumbs are crisp and brown and a meat thermometer inserted into the center of the roast reads 170°F (80°C). This will take about 45 minutes to 1 hour.

Remove the lamb from the oven. Allow it to rest for 15 minutes before slicing.

serves 8 to 10

Stuffed New Potatoes

Baby Carrots with Parsley and Butter

Sautéed Sole with Hazelnuts

Nouvelle Salad Dressings

■ Veal Scallops with Herbs

16 thin veal scallops, about 1¼ pounds (550
    grams) in all
salt to taste, if desired
freshly ground black pepper to taste
6 tablespoons (90 grams) sweet butter
1 tablespoon finely chopped fresh parsley
2 teaspoons finely chopped fresh tarragon or
    ½ teaspoon dried
2 teaspoons finely chopped fresh chives

Lightly pound the veal scallops between
two sheets of waxed paper with a meat
mallet or the side of a heavy knife or cleaver until they are 1-inch (0.5 cm) thick. Season the scallops on both sides with salt
and pepper to taste.

In a large skillet, heat 4 tablespoons (60
grams) of the butter. When the butter is
very hot, add half the scallops and cook
briefly until lightly browned, about 50 to
60 seconds on each side. Remove the veal
to a serving platter and keep warm. Cook
the remaining veal as above.

Melt the remaining butter in the skillet.
Add the parsley, tarragon and chives. Stir
and cook briefly, about 30 seconds. Pour
the sauce over the veal chops on the serving platter and serve immediately.

serves 4

■ Rolled Veal Roast

2 tablespoons (30 grams) sweet butter
2 tablespoons olive oil
3 pounds (1.35 kg) rolled and tied boneless
    veal shoulder or rump (topside) roast
2 carrots, thinly sliced
2 onions, thinly sliced
salt to taste, if desired
freshly ground black pepper to taste
4 parsley sprigs
1 bay leaf
½ teaspoon dried thyme

Preheat the oven to 325°F (170°C).

In a large casserole dish over moderate
heat, melt the butter and oil together.
When the mixture begins to foam, add the
veal. Brown the meat on all sides and
remove it from the casserole to a dish.

Add the carrots and onions to the casserole and sauté until they are slightly
wilted, about 8 to 10 minutes. Add equal
amounts of olive oil and butter if more is
needed.

Return the veal to the casserole. Season
the roast with salt and pepper. Add the
parsley, bay leaf and thyme. Cover the
casserole with aluminum foil and seal
tightly. Roast the veal in the oven until a
meat thermometer inserted into the center of the roast reads 175°F (80°C), about 2
hours.

Remove the veal from the casserole dish
and allow it to rest for 10 minutes on a cutting board before slicing.

Strain the pan juices from the casserole
dish into a saucepan. Skim off all visible
fat and discard the parsley sprigs and bay
leaf. Press the carrots and onion through a
sieve and add the pulp to the saucepan.
Simmer the mixture gently for 2 to 3 minutes. Season the sauce with salt and pepper to taste.

Arrange the veal slices on a serving
platter. Ladle some sauce over each portion before serving.

serves 6

■ Cold Veal Roast with Yogurt Dressing

1 5- to 6-pound (2.25 to 2.7 kg) rolled
  boneless veal shoulder
salt to taste, if desired
freshly ground black pepper to taste
2 medium-sized onions, finely chopped
¼ cup (60 grams) finely chopped fresh
  parsley
1½ tablespoons finely chopped fresh tarragon
  or 1½ teaspoons dried
¾ cup (180 grams) finely chopped fresh
  mushrooms
⅓ cup (75 grams) unflavored bread crumbs
Tangy Yogurt Dressing (see page 24)

Preheat the oven to 350°F (180°C).

Unroll the veal and pound it with a meat mallet or the side of a heavy knife or cleaver until it is flattened into a sheet. Season to taste with salt and pepper.

In a small bowl combine the onions, parsley, tarragon, mushrooms and bread-crumbs. Season with salt and pepper to taste and mix well.

Spread the mixture over the flattened veal. Roll up the veal and tie the roll with white kitchen twine or string at 2-inch (5 cm) intervals. Rub the outside of the roll with freshly ground black pepper.

Put the rolled veal on a rack in a roasting pan and roast until a meat thermometer inserted into the center of the roast reads 175°F (80°C), about 2 hours. Baste the veal with the pan juices every 15 minutes.

Remove the roast from the oven to a serving platter and let cool to room temperature. Cover the roast with aluminum foil and chill for 4 hours or overnight.

Make a double recipe of the yogurt dressing, substituting curry powder for the cumin. Mix well and chill for 4 hours or overnight.

Remove the veal from the refrigerator and let stand at room temperature for 30 minutes. Slice the roast and serve with the yogurt dressing.

serves 8

■ Veal with Ginger Lime Sauce

as served by Derek Hastings

6 tablespoons (90 grams) sweet butter
4 8-ounce (225 grams) boned veal loin chops
  (cutlets)
1 tablespoon very thinly sliced fresh ginger
3 tablespoons fresh lime juice
1 cup (8 fl oz or 240 ml) beef or chicken broth
salt to taste, if desired
freshly ground black pepper to taste
1 lime, quartered

Melt 4 tablespoons (60 grams) of the butter in a skillet over moderate heat. Allow the remaining butter to soften to room temperature.

Add the veal chops to the skillet and cook until they are browned and the edges are dark brown, about 4 to 5 minutes per side. Remove the veal chops from the skillet to a plate and keep warm.

Pour off all but a thin layer of the butter from the skillet. Add the ginger, lime juice and broth. Stir well, scraping the brown bits from the sides and bottom of the skillet, and quickly bring the mixture to a boil. Continue to boil until the sauce is reduced to about ½ cup (4 fl oz or 120 ml), about 3 to 4 minutes. Strain the mixture through a sieve and return the strained sauce to the skillet. Discard any solids remaining in the sieve.

As the strained sauce cooks over low heat, whisk in the remaining butter. Season to taste with salt and pepper. Return the veal chops to the skillet and cook until they are heated through.

To serve, spoon a heaping tablespoon of the sauce onto 4 individual serving plates. Place a veal chop on top of the sauce and spoon additional sauce over each veal chop. Top each veal chop with a lime quarter and serve.

serves 4

■ Veal Scallops with Lemon Sauce

16 thin veal scallops, about 1¼ pounds (550 grams) in all
4 tablespoons (2 fl oz or 60 ml) fresh lemon juice
flour (plain flour) for dredging
3 tablespoons (45 grams) sweet butter
½ cup (4 fl oz or 120 ml) beef broth
2 tablespoons drained capers
1 teaspoon freshly grated lemon rind

Lightly pound the veal scallops between two sheets of waxed paper with a meat mallet or the flat side of a heavy knife or cleaver until they are 1-inch (0.5 cm) thick.

Put the scallops into a shallow dish with 4 teaspoons of the lemon juice. Marinate for 1 hour.

Remove the veal and gently pat dry. Dredge the scallops in flour until they are lightly coated. Shake off any excess flour.

Melt the butter in a heavy skillet over high heat. Add half the veal and cook briefly until lightly browned, about 50 to 60 seconds per side. Remove the scallops to a serving platter and keep warm. Cook the remaining scallops as above.

Add the beef broth to the skillet and cook, stirring well to dissolve all the brown bits from the sides and bottom of the skillet. Continue to cook until the broth is reduced by half. Add the capers, the remaining lemon juice and the grated lemon rind. Stir well. Return the scallops to the skillet, cover, and cook until the veal is tender and heated through, about 2 to 4 minutes. Serve with sauce spooned over each piece of veal.

serves 4

■ Veal Scallops with Papaya and Pistachios

½ cup (120 grams) shelled and skinned pistachio nuts
¼ cup (2 fl oz or 60 ml) hazelnut-flavored liqueur
2 tablespoons olive oil
3 tablespoons (45 grams) sweet butter
24 thin veal scallops, about 2 pounds (900 grams) in all
1 ripe papaya, peeled, seeded and cubed
1 cup (8 fl oz or 240 ml) heavy cream (single cream)
¼ cup (2 fl oz or 60 ml) chicken broth
1 teaspoon grainy mustard
1 tablespoon dry white wine or dry vermouth
chopped fresh mint leaves for garnish

In a small bowl combine the pistachio nuts and hazelnut-flavored liqueur. Soak the nuts for 1 hour, then drain, reserving both the liqueur and the pistachios.

Lightly pound the veal scallops between two sheets of waxed paper with a meat mallet or the side of a heavy knife or cleaver until they are 1-inch (0.5 cm) thick. Season the scallops on both sides with salt and pepper to taste.

Heat the olive oil and 2 tablespoons (30 grams) of the butter together in a large skillet. When the mixture is very hot add half the scallops and cook briefly until lightly browned, about 50 to 60 seconds per side. Remove the scallops to a serving platter and keep warm. Cook the remaining veal as above.

Pour off the fat from the skillet. Add the hazelnut-flavored liqueur and heat gently for about 1 minute. Using a long match, carefully ignite the liqueur. Gently shake the skillet until the flames die out. Pour the liqueur over the veal.

Add the pistachio nuts, papaya, cream, chicken broth, mustard, salt and pepper to the skillet. Quicly bring the mixture to a boil. Continue to boil, stirring constantly, until the sauce is reduced and slightly thickened. Add the wine, stir, and cook for 1 minute longer.

Spoon the sauce over the veal. Garnish with the chopped mint leaves and serve immediately.

serves 6

■ Rolled Veal Scallops with Mustard Sauce

24 thin veal scallops, about 2 pounds (900 grams) in all
1⅔ cups (13 fl oz or 400 ml) water
6 tablespoons (90 grams) wild rice
3 tablespoons (45 grams) sweet butter
3 tablespoons (45 grams) flour (plain flour)
3 cups (24 fl oz or 720 ml) hard apple cider
1½ tablespoons Dijon-style mustard
6 tablespoons (90 grams) sweet butter
½ cup (120 grams) finely chopped onion
½ cup (120 grams) finely chopped seedless green grapes
salt to taste, if desired
freshly ground black pepper to taste
2 tablespoons Calvados or apple brandy
watercress sprigs for garnish

Lightly pound the veal scallops between two sheets of waxed paper with a meat mallet or the flat side of a heavy knife or cleaver until they are ⅛-inch (0.5 cm) thick. Set aside.

Bring the water to the boil in a small saucepan. Add the wild rice and stir. Lower the heat and simmer, covered, until the rice is tender but firm and the water has been absorbed, about 30 minutes. Set aside.

Melt 3 tablespoons (45 grams) of the butter in a saucepan over low heat. Add the flour and cook, stirring constantly, for 3 minutes. Slowly stir in the cider. Raise the heat to moderately high and continue to cook, stirring constantly, until the sauce boils and is thick enough to coat the spoon. If the sauce becomes too thick, add

more cider. Remove from the heat and whisk in the mustard. Continue to whisk until the sauce is well blended. Set aside.

In a skillet, melt 2 tablespoons (30 grams) of the butter over moderately high heat. Add the onion and cook until soft but not brown, about 5 minutes. Remove the skillet from the heat and allow the mixture to cool. Add the wild rice, grapes and 1 tablespoon of the sauce. Season to taste with salt and pepper and mix well.

Preheat the oven to 350°F (180°C). Butter an 8 × 12-inch (20 × 30 cm) baking dish.

Place a heaping tablespoon of the wild rice mixture onto the center of each veal scallop. Spread the mixture evenly over the scallop, leaving a thin border. Roll up the scallops and tie them with white kitchen string or twine.

Melt the remaining butter in a large skillet over medium-high heat. Quickly brown the veal rolls on all sides in the butter. Put the veal rolls into the prepared baking dish.

Pour off all the fat from the skillet. Add the Calvados or apple brandy and cook, stirring well to dissolve all the brown bits clinging to the sides and bottom of the pan. Pour the Calvados or apple brandy over the veal rolls.

Top the veal rolls with the reserved cider and mustard sauce. Bake the veal rolls until tender, about 20 minutes.

To serve, transfer the veal rolls to a serving platter and top with some of the sauce. Garnish with watercress sprigs and serve the remaining sauce in a sauceboat on the side.

serves 6

■ Paul Prudhomme's Breaded Veal with Czarina Sauce

6 4-ounce (120 grams) veal cutlets, without
   bone
2¼ teaspoons salt
1¼ teaspoons sweet paprika
2 teaspoons minced onion
½ teaspoon cayenne pepper
¼ teaspoon freshly ground black pepper
1 garlic clove, minced
¼ teaspoon dry mustard
¾ cup (110 grams) flour (plain flour)
6 tablespoons (90 grams) sweet butter
4 tablespoons olive oil
¾ cup (180 grams) julienned onion
¾ cup (180 grams) julienned zucchini
   (courgette)
¾ cup (180 grams) julienned yellow squash
1½ teaspoons fresh lemon juice
1 cup (8 fl oz or 240 ml) heavy cream (single
   cream)
¼ pound (120 grams) small shrimp, peeled,
   cleaned and deveined
¼ cup (60 grams) finely grated Parmesan
   cheese

Lightly pound the veal cutlets between two sheets of waxed paper with a meat mallet or the flat side of a heavy knife or cleaver until the cutlets are about ¼-inch (1 cm) thick.

In a small bowl combine the salt, paprika, minced onion, cayenne pepper, black pepper, garlic and dry mustard. Mix well. Sprinkle ¼ teaspoon of the mixture over each of the cutlets. Combine 1 tablespoon of the mixture with the flour in a shallow plate or pan.

Dredge the veal in the seasoned flour and shake off any excess.

In a large skillet over high heat melt 2 tablespoons (30 grams) of the butter together with 2 tablespoons of the olive oil. Add half the veal to the skillet and cook briefly until lightly browned, about 1 minute per side. Remove the veal to a serving platter and keep warm.

Pour off the fat from the skillet and wipe it clean. Using 2 more tablespoons (30 grams) of the butter and 2 more of the olive oil, cook the remaining veal as above, but do not pour off the fat when done. Put the platter with the veal into a cool (200°F, 95°C) oven to keep warm.

Add the onion, zucchini (courgette) and yellow squash to the skillet and sauté over high heat until they begin to soften, about 2 minutes. Add the lemon juice, remaining butter, remaining seasoning mixture and cream. Cook, stirring occasionally, until the mixture simmers. Add the shrimp and cook for 1 minute longer, stirring frequently. Add the grated cheese and continue to cook until the shrimp are done, about 2 minutes longer. If the sauce begins to separate, add 1 to 2 tablespoons of water and stir until smooth.

Transfer the reserved veal to individual serving plates. Top each serving with some of the sauce and serve at once.

serves 6

■ Calf's Liver in Mocha and Red Wine Sauce

4 6-ounce (180 grams) slices fresh calf's liver
3 garlic cloves, finely chopped
2 tablespoons olive oil
4 onions, thinly sliced
1 cup (8 fl oz or 240 ml) dry red wine
2 cups (16 fl oz or 480 ml) freshly brewed
   strong coffee
24 small button mushrooms
salt to taste, if desired
freshly ground black pepper to taste

Rub each liver slice on both sides with garlic, salt and pepper. Set aside.

Heat the olive oil in a skillet over medium high heat. When the oil is hot, add the onions and sauté, stirring constantly, until golden, about 8 minutes. Add the wine and coffee to the skillet. Cook until the liquid is reduced by one-third. Add the mushrooms to the mixture and bring it to a simmer. Continue to simmer, stirring frequently, for 5 minutes.

Add the liver slices to the skillet and cook over low heat until the liver is brown on the outside but still slightly pink on the inside, about 12 to 15 minutes. Turn the slices occasionally.

Put the liver slices on a serving platter and spoon the sauce over them. Serve immediately.

serves 4

■ Calf's Liver in Orange Sauce

2 cups (16 fl oz or 480 ml) dry red wine
1 tablespoon olive oil
¼ teaspoon crumbled dried tarragon
freshly ground black pepper to taste
1 pound (450 grams) fresh calf's liver, very thinly sliced
3 tablespoons (45 grams) sweet butter
zest of 1 medium-sized orange, cut into thin strips
salt to taste, if desired

In a shallow bowl or dish combine the wine, oil, garlic, tarragon and pepper. Mix well and add the liver slices, turning often until the slices are evenly coated. Cover the dish and marinate at room temperature for 3 hours.

Drain the liver well and reserve the marinade.

In a skillet, melt the butter over moderately high heat. Add the liver and sauté until lightly browned on the outside but still pink on the inside, about 2 to 3 minutes per side. Remove the liver from the skillet to a plate and keep warm. Pour off the remaining butter from the skillet.

Add the reserved marinade and the orange zest to the skillet. Bring the mixture to a boil. Continue to boil until the liquid is reduced by half.

Return the liver to the skillet. Cook until the liver is just heated through, no longer than 1 minute. Season to taste with salt and serve at once.

serves 4

■ Rabbit Roasted with Rosemary

as adapted from Craig Claiborne

1 2- to 2½-pound (900 grams to 1.12 kg) cleaned young rabbit
salt to taste, if desired
freshly ground black pepper to taste
2 tablespoons olive oil
2 tablespoons (30 grams) sweet butter
1 teaspoon finely ground dried rosemary
2 tablespoons minced shallots
1 teaspoon finely chopped garlic
½ cup (4 fl oz or 120 ml) dry white wine
½ cup (4 fl oz or 120 ml) chicken broth
¼ cup (60 grams) finely chopped parsley

Preheat the oven to 450°F (230°C).

Cut the rabbit into serving pieces and season to taste with salt and pepper.

In a baking dish large enough to hold the rabbit pieces in one layer, heat the olive oil and 1 tablespoon (15 grams) of the butter. Add the rabbit pieces and sprinkle them with the rosemary.

Bake the rabbit for 30 minutes. Turn the pieces and bake for 5 minutes longer. Sprinkle the pieces with the shallots and garlic and bake for 5 minutes longer. Add the wine and chicken broth and bake for 20 minutes longer, turning the pieces twice. Add the remaining butter to the baking dish and stir. Remove the dish from the oven and sprinkle with the chopped parsley. Serve the rabbit directly from the baking dish with the sauce.

serves 4

Grains and Pasta

Nothing is quite as satisfying as a plate of pasta. Whether sauced with nothing more than oil and garlic or bathed in butter and cream and tuffles, the filling qualities of pasta would be hard to equal. Yet by itself, pasta is not particularly fattening. The sauce is usually the culprit.

The Futurist Marinetti, between the wars, tried to stamp out the Italian love of pasta through a book he called *La Cucina Futuristica*. Considering the surge in pasta consumption since then, he didn't even come close to the mark. Pasta is cheap, filling, infinitely variable in shape and size and capable of assuming thousands of different disguises, depending on what is placed on top of it or mixed with it. It can be as light as a spring day or as warming as a roaring fire on a bitter winter's evening. It cooks quickly, whether fresh or dried. Pasta has become the most versatile food in the kitchen.

Other grain foods can be equally interesting. Rice, barley, sweet corn, buckwheat (kasha) and bulgur all repay experimentation. Rice, of course, is the mainstay of a large part of the world's population. It comes in a bewildering number of varieties besides the white long grain so familiar in the West. The *arborio* rice of Piedmont in Northern Italy is a necessity for risotto, with the grains cooking up creamy yet separate. The sticky rice of Japan is useful for many dishes where the need to hold things together becomes imperative. The list could go on. Like pasta, rice can be used at any place in the meal, but it must be cooked with precision. Otherwise, you will end up with a glutinous mess.

The other grains should be tried also. Barley makes a wonderful casserole. Corn can be used for fritters, soups, breads and griddlecakes. Bulgur can be combined in salads—the Lebanese tabouli—with meats and vegetables. Couscous should not be forgotten. Just because you are not familiar with a particular grain, do not ignore it. They can open up whole new worlds of taste sensations.

■ Lemon Rice with Capers

1 cup (225 grams) long-grain white rice
3 tablespoons (45 grams) sweet butter
salt to taste, if desired
freshly ground black pepper to taste
2 tablespoons fresh lemon juice
1 tablespoon rinsed and drained capers
1 teaspoon finely grated lemon rind

Bring 4 cups (1¾ pints or 1 litre) water to a boil in a large saucepan. Add the rice and cook over high heat, stirring often, until the rice is just tender, about 15 minutes. Remove the rice from the heat and drain in a colander. Rinse with cold running water and drain well.

Melt 1 tablespoon (15 grams) of the butter in a large skillet over low heat. Add the rice, salt and pepper. Heat the rice, fluffing it with a fork. When the rice is hot, add the lemon juice, capers and lemon rind. Stir gently for 5 seconds, then remove skillet from the heat. Add the remaining butter and stir gently. Transfer to a serving dish and serve at once.

serves 6

■ Arborio Rice with Asparagus

½ cup (120 grams) pine nuts (pignoli)
1 pound (450 grams) fresh asparagus
4 cups (1¾ pints or 1 litre) chicken broth
1 cup (225 grams) dry white wine
¼ cup (60 grams) sweet butter
1 onion, finely chopped
1½ cups (340 grams) Italian arborio rice
  (short-grained rice)
½ cup (120 grams) freshly grated Parmesan
  cheese
salt to taste, if desired
freshly ground black pepper to taste

Toast the pine nuts in a skillet over moderate heat until lightly browned, about 5 minutes. Shake the pan frequently. Remove the skillet from the heat and set aside.

Snap off the tough ends of the asparagus stalks and peel the stalks, if desired. Slice the stalks into ½-inch (1.5 cm) pieces, leaving the tips whole. Set aside.

Combine the chicken broth and white wine in a saucepan. Bring the mixture to a simmer over low heat.

As the broth and white wine heat, melt the butter in a saucepan over moderate heat. Add the onion and sauté, stirring often, until lightly browned, about 5 minutes.

Add the rice to the saucepan and stir until the grains are well coated with the butter and onion mixture. Pour in just enough of the hot broth and white wine mixture to barely cover the rice. Reduce the heat and simmer gently, uncovered, until the liquid is almost gone and the mixture is thick, about 3 to 5 minutes. Stir frequently. Repeat this procedure, adding only enough of the broth and white wine to barely cover the rice, until the rice is tender but still firm. In all, this should take about 25 minutes.

When the rice has about 10 minutes longer to cook, add the asparagus stalk pieces and stir. When the rice has about 5 minutes longer to cook, add the asparagus tips and stir.

Remove the rice from the heat. Add the reserved pine nuts, Parmesan cheese, salt and pepper. Mix gently. Transfer to a bowl and serve immediately.

serves 6

■ Saffron Rice

½ teaspoon saffron threads
¼ cup (2 fl oz or 60 ml) water
¼ cup (60 grams) sweet butter
1½ cup (340 grams) long-grain white rice
2¾ cup (22 fl oz or 660 ml) boiling water
salt to taste, if desired

Put the saffron threads into a small bowl. Add the ¼ cup (2 fl oz or 60 ml) water and dissolve the saffron.

Melt the butter in a large saucepan over moderate heat. Add the rice and cook, stirring constantly, until all the grains are well coated with the butter. Add the saffron and water, the boiling water and salt. Quickly bring the mixture to a boil. Reduce the heat and cover the saucepan. Simmer gently until all the liquid has been absorbed and the rice is tender, about 20 minutes. Stir often.

Transfer the rice to a serving bowl and serve at once.

serves 4

■ Rice with Pistachios and Pine Nuts

1 cup (225 grams) long-grain white rice
1 cup (8 fl oz or 240 ml) water
1 cup (8 fl oz or 240 ml) chicken broth
¼ cup (60 grams) shelled pistachio nuts
½ cup (120 grams) pine nuts (pignoli) or
*   toasted slivered almonds*
3 tablespoons (45 grams) sweet butter
1 teaspoon powdered mace
salt to taste, if desired

Bring the water and chicken broth to a boil in a saucepan. Add the rice, stir, and cover the saucepan. Reduce the heat and simmer until the rice is tender and all the liquid is absorbed, about 20 minutes.

While the rice cooks, melt the butter in a heavy skillet. Add the pistachios and pine nuts and cook, stirring frequently, until the nuts are golden, about 3 to 5 minutes.

Add the rice to the skillet with the nuts. Season with the mace and salt. Stir until well blended and heated through. Serve at once.

serves 4 to 6

■ Wild Rice Pancakes with Nuts

1 cup (225 grams) blanched almonds
⅓ cup (75 grams) wild rice
1 cup (8 fl oz or 240 ml) water
salt to taste, if desired
2 cups (16 fl oz or 480 ml) milk
2 tablespoons (30 grams) sweet butter
1 teaspoon salt
4 egg yolks
4 egg whites
1 cup (225 grams) flour (plain flour)
¼ teaspoon cream of tartar
1 tablespoon (15 grams) or more sweet butter
1 tablespoon or more vegetable oil

Toast the almonds in a dry skillet over moderate heat until lightly browned, about 5 to 8 minutes. Shake the skillet frequently. Remove the skillet from the heat and cool. When cool enough to handle, chop the nuts very finely. Set aside.

Rinse the wild rice in a sieve under cold running water for 2 to 3 minutes. Drain thoroughly.

Put the water and salt to taste into a saucepan and bring to a boil. Add the wild rice and lower the heat. Cover the saucepan and simmer until the rice is tender and all the water is absorbed, about 45 to 60 minutes.

Add the milk, melted butter and additional salt to taste to the wild rice. Stir until well blended.

Beat the egg yolks in a mixing bowl until they are a light lemony color, about 3 minutes. Add the yolks to the wild rice mixture and mix well. Add the chopped almonds and the flour and stir until well blended.

In another mixing bowl, beat the egg whites with the cream of tartar until they are stiff but not dry. Carefully fold the beaten egg whites into the rice mixture.

Preheat the oven to 180°F (80°C).

Melt the butter and olive oil together in a large skillet or on a large griddle. In batches, spoon 2½-inch (6.5 cm) pancakes of the wild rice mixture onto the skillet. Cook over moderate heat until the bottoms of the pancakes are golden brown and the pancakes begin to set, about 2 to 3 minutes. Carefully turn the pancakes with a spatula and brown the other side. Put the finished pancakes in a single layer on a baking sheet and keep warm in the oven as the rest of the pancakes are cooked. Add additional butter and olive oil to the skillet as needed.

Serve the pancakes with melted butter or sour cream for toppings.

serves 6 to 8

■ Wild Rice with Butter

⅔ cup (150 grams) wild rice
¼ cup (60 grams) sweet butter
salt to taste, if desired
freshly ground black pepper to taste

Put the wild rice in a sieve and rinse under cold running water for 2 to 3 minutes. Drain well.

Put the wild rice in a saucepan and add enough cold water to cover the rice to a depth of 3 inches (8 cm). Bring the water to a boil. Reduce the heat and simmer, uncovered, until the wild rice is tender but still firm. Stir often. Remove the saucepan from the heat and drain the colander. Do not rinse.

Melt the butter in a saucepan over medium heat. Add the wild rice and cook, stirring constantly, until it is just heated through, about 2 to 3 minutes. Season with salt and pepper. Transfer to a serving bowl and serve at once.

serves 4

■ Two-Rice Salad

¾ cup (180 grams) well-rinsed wild rice
¾ cup (180 grams) well-rinsed brown rice
¼ cup (2 fl oz or 60 ml) red wine vinegar
½ cup (4 fl oz or 120 ml) olive oil
12 pimento-stuffed green olives, sliced
⅓ cup (75 grams) finely chopped scallions or chives

Add the wild rice to a large saucepan of boiling water. Stir well and boil for 15 minutes.

Add the brown rice to the wild rice. Stir well and boil for 15 minutes longer. Drain the rice into a colander and rinse well under cold running water.

Put the rice into a steamer and steam, covered, until dry and fluffy, about 15 to 20 minutes. Put the rice into a large serving bowl.

In a small mixing bowl, combine the vinegar, salt and pepper. In a slow, steady stream, whisk in the olive oil. Continue to whisk until the dressing is smooth and well blended.

Pour the dressing over the rice and toss until well coated. Add the olives, scallions and additional salt and pepper if desired. Toss gently but well. Let the salad cool and serve at room temperature.

serves 6

Pasta

■ Green Noodles with Vegetables and Goat Cheese

as adapted from Diane Rossen Worthington

2 cups (450 grams) broccoli flowerettes
2 cups (450 grams) cauliflower flowerettes
1½ cups (12 fl oz or 360 ml) chicken broth
8 ounces (225 grams) goat cheese (chèvre)
2 teaspoons finely chopped fresh thyme or 1
    teaspoon dried
salt to taste, if desired
¾ pound (340 grams) spinach fettucini or
    noodles

Cook the broccoli and cauliflower flowerettes in boiling water to cover until tender but still crisp. Drain in a colander and rinse with cold water. Drain well again and set aside.

Bring the chicken broth to a boil in a skillet. Continue to boil until it is reduced to 1 cup (8 fl oz or 240 ml).

Carefully remove the rind from the goat cheese. Cut the cheese into small pieces. Sprinkle the pieces over the chicken broth and whisk until well blended. Add the thyme, salt and pepper. Simmer over low heat until the sauce thickens slightly, about 5 minutes. Add the broccoli and cauliflower flowerettes and stir. Remove the skillet from the heat and keep warm.

Cook the fettucini or noodles *al dente* in a large pot of boiling salted water. Drain well in a colander. Add the fettucini to the skillet with the sauce and toss until well mixed. Transfer the mixture to a serving bowl, sprinkle with the watercress and serve at once.

serves 4

■ Fettucini with Fresh Roe

as served by Derek Hastings

4 tablespoons olive oil
½ pound (225 grams) ripe tomatoes, peeled,
    seeded and chopped
2 garlic cloves, finely chopped
½ pound (225 grams) fresh flounder, shad or
    any soft roe
salt to taste, if desired
freshly ground black pepper to taste
¾ pound (340 grams) fettucini
2 tablespoons heavy cream (single cream)
2 tablespoons finely chopped parsley

Heat the 4 tablespoons olive oil in a large skillet. Add the tomatoes and garlic and sauté over moderate heat until the tomatoes are softened, about 8 to 10 minutes.

Add the roe to the skillet and cook over moderately low heat until the roe begin to get firm, about 10 minutes. Gently break up the roe with a wooden spoon. Season with salt and pepper.

Cook the fettucini in a large pot of boiling salted water until it is *al dente*. Drain well. Transfer the fettucini to a serving dish and toss with the 2 teaspoons olive oil.

Add the cream to the skillet with the roe. Stir in the parsley. Pour the sauce over the fettucini. Toss gently but well and serve at once, with the peppermill on the table.

serves 4

■ Fettucini with Broccoli Purée

2 pound (900 grams) broccoli
1½ cups (12 fl oz or 360 ml) heavy cream
  (single cream)
3 tablespoons (45 grams) softened sweet
  butter
2 large shallots, finely chopped
salt to taste, if desired
freshly ground black pepper to taste
⅛ teaspoon grated nutmeg
¾ pound (340 grams) fettucini

Break the broccoli into flowerettes. Set aside 16 of the flowerettes. Peel the large main stalks and cut them into ¾-inch (2 cm) pieces.

Bring a large saucepan of lightly salted water to a boil. Add the broccoli stalk slices to the water and boil for 2 minutes. Add the flowerettes and boil rapidly until the stems and flowerettes are just tender, about 5 minutes. Drain in a colander and rinse with cold water. Drain well again.

In batches, put the cooked broccoli into the container of a food processor or blender. Add 4 tablespoons of the cream, a little at a time, and purée until smooth.

Heat 1 tablespoon (15 grams) of the butter in a saucepan. Add the shallots and sauté until soft but not brown, about 5 to 7 minutes. Add the puréed broccoli to the saucepan and stir. Slowly stir in the remaining cream. Add the salt, pepper and nutmeg. Stir and keep warm over very low heat. Do not let the mixture boil.

Cook the fettucini in a large pot of boiling salted water until it is *al dente*. Drain well and transfer to a serving dish.

While the fettucini cooks, blanch the reserved broccoli flowerettes in a saucepan of boiling water for 2 minutes. Drain well.

Add the remaining butter to the broccoli sauce. Pour the sauce over the fettucini and toss gently but well. Garnish with the blanched flowerettes and serve at once.

serves 4 to 6

■ Fettucini with Scallop Seviche

½ pound (225 grams) carrots, peeled and
  julienned
½ cup (4 fl oz or 120 ml) dry vermouth
⅓ cup (3 fl oz or 80 ml) olive oil
1½ teaspoons finely chopped fresh marjoram
  or ½ teaspoon crumbled dried marjoram
1½ teaspoons finely chopped fresh thyme or
  ½ teaspoon crumbled dried thyme
salt to taste, if desired
½ teaspoon crushed coriander seed
½ teaspoon finely chopped garlic
⅛ teaspoon dried hot red pepper flakes
½ pound (225 grams) onions, thinly sliced
1 pound (450 grams) fresh sea scallops,
  quartered
¼ cup (2 fl oz or 60 ml) fresh lemon juice
¼ cup (60 grams) finely chopped parsley
2 tablespoons chopped fresh chives
freshly ground black pepper to taste
2 teaspoons olive oil
¾ pound (340 grams) fettucini

In a large saucepan combine the carrots, vermouth, ⅓ cup (3 fl oz or 80 ml), olive oil, marjoram, thyme, salt, coriander, garlic and hot red pepper flakes. Bring the mixture to a simmer, cover, and cook for 5 minutes. Add the onions and simmer until the carrots and onions are tender but still crisp, about 5 minutes longer. Transfer the mixture to a large nonmetal mixing bowl and let cool to room temperature.

Add the scallops, lemon juice, parsely, chives, and a generous amount of black pepper to the cooled carrot mixture. Stir well to blend thoroughly. Cover the bowl and refrigerate for 12 hours or overnight. The scallops will "cook" in the mixture and turn opaque when they are "done."

Cook the fettucini in a large pot of boiling salted water until it is *al dente*. Drain well. Transfer the fettucini to a serving dish and toss lightly with the 2 teaspoons olive oil. Let the pasta cool to room temperature.

Remove the scallops mixture from the

refrigerator and let it come to room temperature. Pour the scallops over the fettucini and toss gently but well. Serve at room temperature.

serves 4 to 6

■ Pasta with Sweetbreads and Ginger Sauce

1 pound (450 grams) veal sweetbreads
1½ teaspoons salt
2 tablespoons (30 grams) sweet butter
½ cup (120 grams)finely chopped onion
½ cup (120 grams) finely chopped carrot
½ cup (120 grams) finely chopped leek, white part only
½ cup (120 grams) chopped mushrooms
¼ cup (60 grams) finely chopped celery
1 bay leaf
1 fresh thyme sprig or ½ teaspoon crumbled dried thyme
salt to taste, if desired
freshly ground black pepper to taste
1 tablespoon (15 grams) sweet butter
2 tablespoons minced shallot
2½ cups (20 fl oz or 600 ml) dry white wine
¼ cup (60 grams) hazelnuts
2 cups (16 fl oz or 480 ml) heavy cream (single cream)
2 tablespoons finely chopped fresh ginger
1 pound (450 grams) fettucini or linguini
4 tablespoons (60 grams) softened sweet butter

Rinse the sweetbreads and put them in a bowl with enough cold water to cover. Sprinkle with ½ teaspoon salt and cover the bowl. Soak the sweetbreads overnight in the refrigerator, changing the water and adding ½ teaspoon salt twice.

Toast the hazelnuts in a skillet until they are lightly browned, about 5 minutes. Remove the hazelnuts from the skillet and put them on a clean kitchen towel. Rub the nuts in the towel to remove the skins. Chop the hazelnuts and set aside.

Drain the sweetbreads well and put them in a saucepan. Add enough cold water to cover them to a depth of 2 inches (5 cm). Bring the water to a simmer and gently cook the sweetbreads for 5 minutes. Drain well, reserving 2½ cups (20 fl oz or 600 ml) of the cooking liquid. Rinse the sweetbreads under cold water. Peel off and discard the thin membrane. Set the sweetbreads aside.

In a large skillet, melt 2 tablespoons (30 grams) of the butter over low heat. Add the onions, carrots, leeks, mushrooms and celery. Sauté until the vegetables are just softened, about 5 minutes. Add the sweetbreads, the reserved cooking liquid, and the bay leaf, thyme, salt and pepper. Stir, cover the saucepan, and cook over low heat until the sweetbreads are tender, about 45 minutes. Turn the sweetbreads once as they cook.

When done, remove the sweetbreads from the saucepan with a slotted spoon. Put them on a plate and keep warm.

Strain the liquid and vegetables in the saucepan through a sieve. Press the vegetables with the back of a spoon to remove all the liquid to the saucepan. Cook the liquid over high heat until it is reduced by half. Set aside.

In another saucepan, melt 1 tablespoon (15 grams) of the butter over moderate heat. Add the shallots and sauté until translucent, about 3 minutes. Add the wine. Raise the heat to high and cook until the liquid is reduced by half. Add the chopped hazelnuts to the saucepan and cook until the liquid is almost gone.

Add the reserved cooking liquid and the cream to the saucepan. Cook until the mixture is reduced by half. Strain any solids remaining in the saucepan. Add the ginger and cook for 2 minutes over low heat. Strain the sauce again, discarding any solids remaining in the sieve. Keep the sauce warm.

Cook the pasta in a large pot of boiling water until it is *al dente*. Drain well and return the pasta to the pot. Toss with the 4 tablespoons (60 grams) of softened butter. Transfer the pasta to a serving platter.

Slice the reserved sweetbreads very thinly. Arrange the sweetbreads on top of the pasta. Spoon the sauce over the sweetbreads and pasta and serve.

serves 6

■ Pasta with Ricotta and Caviar

4 tablespoons (60 grams) sweet butter
2 tablespoons (30 grams) fresh ricotta cheese
2 tablespoons heavy cream (single cream)
freshly ground black pepper to taste
¾ pound (340 grams) linguini
¼ cup (60 grams) caviar

Melt the butter in a large skillet. Add the ricotta, cream and very generous amount of black pepper. Stir and cook over moderately low heat for 2 minutes.

Cook the linguini in a large pot of boiling salted water until it is *al dente*. Drain well, reserving 2 tablespoons of the cooking water.

Add the caviar to the cream mixture in the skillet. Stir well until smooth.

Add the drained linguini to the skillet. Add the reserved cooking water and cook, stirring constantly, for 1 minute.

Transfer to a serving dish and serve at once.

serves 4

■ Pasta with Uncooked Tomato Sauce

4 large ripe tomatoes, at room temperature
½ cup (120 grams) sliced, pitted (stoned) olives
½ cup (120 grams) chopped fresh basil
1 tablespoon chopped fresh parsley
5 garlic cloves, finely chopped
½ teaspoon hot red pepper flakes
salt to taste, if desired

freshly ground black pepper to taste
½ cup (4 fl oz or 120 ml) olive oil
1 pound (450 grams) vermicelli or thin spaghetti

Coarsely chop the tomatoes and put them into a large nonmetal bowl. Add the olives, basil, parsley, garlic, red pepper flakes, salt and pepper. Stir until well mixed. Add the olive oil and toss gently. Let the mixture stand at room temperature for 2 hours to blend the flavors. Toss occasionally.

Cook the pasta in a large pot of boiling water until it is *al dente*. Drain well.

Put the pasta into a large serving bowl. Pour the tomato mixture over the pasta and toss gently but well. Serve at once.

serves 4 to 6

■ Pasta Salad with Broccoli, Tomatoes and Olives

1 pound (450 grams) corkscrew-shaped pasta (fusili)
2 tablespoons olive oil
1 large head broccoli, broken into flowerettes
2 large tomatoes, peeled, seeded, and chopped
1 cup (225 grams) sliced, pitted black (stoned) olives
Parmesan Dressing:
2 tablespoons red wine vinegar
2 garlic cloves, finely chopped
4 tablespoons chopped fresh basil
salt to taste, if desired
freshly ground black pepper to taste
4 tablespoons olive oil
½ cup (120 grams) freshly grated Parmesan cheese

Cook the pasta in boiling water with 1 tablespoon olive oil. When pasta is just *al dente*, drain well and rinse with cold water to cool. Drain well again and put the pasta into a large serving bowl. Add 1 tablespoon olive oil and toss well.

Cook the broccoli in a saucepan of boiling water until just tender, about 3 minutes. Drain and rinse with cold water.

Drain well again. Add the broccoli to the pasta.

Add the tomatoes and olives to the pasta. Toss well.

In a small mixing bowl, combine the vinegar, garlic, basil, salt and pepper. Whisk until well blended. In a slow, steady stream, whisk in the olive oil. Add the cheese and continue to whisk until the dressing is smooth and well blended.

Pour the dressing over the pasta mixture and toss well. Serve the salad at room temperature.

serves 4

■ Pasta with Cheese, Pistachios and Cognac

as served by Derek Hastings

2 tablespoons shelled pistachio nuts
boiling water
¾ pound (340 grams) small pasta shells or
  any other shape
½ cup (120 grams) sweet butter
3 ounces (35 grams) sweet young Gorgonzola
  cheese
½ cup (4 fl oz or 120 ml) milk
salt to taste, if desired
freshly ground black pepper to taste
2 tablespoons Cognac or brandy

Put the pistachios into a small bowl and add enough boiling water to cover. Soak the nuts for 2 minutes and then drain. Peel the skins off the nuts. Put the nuts into the container of a food processor or blender and process until fine. Set aside.

Cook the pasta in a large pot of boiling water until it is *al dente*. Drain well and transfer to a serving bowl.

While the pasta cooks, melt the butter and the cheese in a heavy saucepan over low heat. Stir frequently. When the butter and cheese have melted together, add the milk and cook, stirring constantly, over very low heat for 5 minutes. Season to taste with salt and pepper.

Remove the saucepan from the heat

and add the reserved pistachios and the Cognac. Stir to mix well. Pour the sauce over the pasta and serve at once.

serves 4

■ Pasta Salad with Seafood

1 pound (450 grams) small pasta shells
2 tablespoons olive oil
¼ pound (120 grams) snow peas, thinly
  sliced
1 sweet red pepper, thinly sliced
1 pound (450 grams) shelled cooked shrimp
1 small red onion, thinly sliced
1 cup (225 grams) pitted (stoned) whole black
  olives
½ pound (225 grams) shredded cooked
  crabmeat
Dill and Lemon Dressing:
3 tablespoons chopped fresh dill or 1½
  teaspoons dried dill
2 garlic cloves, minced
½ cup (4 fl oz or 120 ml) fresh lemon juice
½ cup (4 fl oz or 120 ml) olive oil
salt to taste, if desired
freshly ground black pepper to taste

Cook the pasta in boiling water with 1 tablespoon olive oil. When pasta is just *al dente*, drain well and rinse with cold water to cool. Drain well again and put the pasta into a large serving bowl. Add 1 tablespoon olive oil and toss well.

Cook the snow pea and red pepper strips in a small saucepan of boiling water until just tender, about 1 minute. Drain well and rinse with cold water. Drain well again and add to the pasta.

Add the shrimp, onion, olives and crabmeat to the pasta. Toss well.

In a small mixing bowl combine the dill, garlic and lemon juice. Whisk until well blended. In a slow, steady stream whisk in the olive oil. Continue to whisk until the dressing is smooth and well blended. Add the salt and pepper and whisk again. Pour the dressing over the pasta mixture and toss until the ingredients are well coated. Serve at once.

serves 6

■ Shrimp-Filled Pasta Shells

2 pounds (900 grams) shrimp (prawns), cleaned, peeled and deveined
3 egg whites
1 cup (8 fl oz or 240 ml) heavy cream (single cream)
juice of 1 lemon
⅓ cup (3 fl oz or 80 ml) light or white rum
salt to taste, if desired
4 whole scallions (green onions), minced
36 cooked and drained large pasta shells
1½ pounds (675 grams) shredded mozzarella cheese
chopped chives for garnish

Put the shrimp and egg whites into the container of a food processor or blender and process until a smooth paste is formed.

Empty the mixture into a bowl and add the cream, lemon juice, rum and salt. Stir until the mixture is smooth. Fold in the scallions (green onions). Cover the bowl and chill for 2 hours.

Preheat the oven to 350°F (180°C).

Remove the shrimp mixture from the refrigerator. Using a teaspoon, fill the pasta shells with the mixture. Put the shells side by side in a single layer in a shallow, buttered baking dish. Top with the mozzarella cheese.

Bake until the cheese· is melted and golden, about 20 to 25 minutes. Sprinkle with the chopped chives and serve.

serves 6

■ Oriental Noodle Salad

8 ounces (225 grams) linguini
2 tablespoons olive oil
10 whole scallions (green onions), thinly sliced
6 cherry tomatoes, halved and seeded
2 large broccoli stalks, peeled and very thinly sliced
Soy Sauce Dressing:
½ cup (4 fl oz or 120 ml) soy sauce
½ cup (4 fl oz or 120 ml) olive oil
1 garlic clove, finely chopped
Tabasco sauce to taste
3 tablespoons fresh lemon juice

Cook the linguini in boiling water with 1 tablespoon olive oil. When linguini is just *al dente*, drain well and rinse with cold water to cool. Drain well again and put the linguini into a large serving bowl. Add 1 tablespoon olive oil and toss well.

Add the scallions, tomatoes and broccoli to the linguini. Toss well.

In a small mixing bowl combine the soy sauce, ½ cup (120 grams) olive oil, garlic, Tabasco sauce and lemon juice. Whisk until dressing is smooth and well blended. Pour the dressing over the linguini mixture and toss until well coated. Chill for at least 2 hours before serving.

serves 6

Glazed Ham with Apricots

Goat Cheese and Chives Soufflés

Veal Scallops with Mustard Sauce

Chicken Sauteed with Lemon and Herbs

Glazed Poached Pears

Vegetables

The bounty of the earth has until recently suffered the indignity of being overcooked and then either slathered with butter or drowned in floury cream sauces. Nothing is as delicate as a fresh picked vegetable, nor as prone to damage. From the moment of picking, a vegetable begins to lose vitamins and flavor. The new cuisine treats vegetables the way a jeweler handles a perfect stone...with reverence and care. Vegetables are cooked only until they are tender but still resilient. Never, never should you encounter a limp carrot or mushy peas. Furthermore, since vegetables provide most of the color on the plate, every caution should be taken to preserve their natural colors. In turn, lightly cooked vegetables provide an outlet for the cook's natural artistry in arrangement.

The new cuisine has been particularly successful in creating new and unusual combinations of vegetables, bringing new flavors to light along the way. Squash with fennel and leek, warm asparagus with hazelnuts, a perfect steamed potato with a mild garlic purée are some of the possibilities. These can actually be served on their own, separate from the meat course. In France and Italy this is the norm, and on a warm day the meat course can easily be dispensed with altogether.

Perhaps the best ways to cook vegetables, especially green and leafy ones, are to steam them gently or sauté them. The natural flavors are preserved, and with just the slightest touch of fresh herbs, butter and perhaps a spoonful of fresh cream, you can be proud to present the vegetable on any occasion.

Certain common vegetables can be made more appealing through careful buying. A freshly dug potato or carrot has recognizable taste, unlike the woody monsters sometimes seen in markets. In fact, the smaller the vegetable, the more delicate and appealing the taste, especially roots and tubers. It may be impressive to see a marrow or zucchini four feet long, but the taste will resemble nothing so much as bland cellulose.

All in all, vegetables add texture, taste and visual excitement to a meal. Treat them as allies, not enemies.

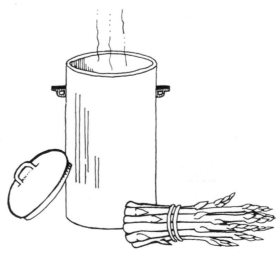

■ Warm Asparagus with Hazelnut Dressing

½ cup (120 grams) hazelnuts
3 tablespoons hazelnut oil
3 tablespoons olive oil
2 tablespoons white wine or tarragon vinegar
salt to taste, if desired
freshly ground black pepper to taste
1½ pounds (700 grams) fresh asparagus

Preheat the oven to 350°F (180°C).

Put the hazelnuts on a baking sheet or in a shallow baking pan. Toast the nuts in the oven for 10 minutes. Remove the nuts from the oven and put them on a clean kitchen towel. Rub the skins from the nuts with towel. Coarsely chop the nuts and set aside.

In a large bowl combine the hazelnut oil, olive oil, vinegar, salt and pepper. Whisk until well blended. Let the dressing stand at room temperature to blend the flavors.

Trim and peel the bottoms of the asparagus stalks. Cook the asparagus in boiling water to cover until just tender, about 5 to 8 minutes. Using a slotted spoon, remove the stalks from the water and drain them on paper towels.

Arrange the asparagus in a serving dish. Spoon the dressing over the asparagus and sprinkle with the hazelnuts.

serves 4

■ Broccoli and Roasted Red Pepper with Garlic

1 large sweet red pepper
2½ pounds (1.125 kg) fresh broccoli, trimmed into spears
salt to taste, if desired
3 garlic cloves, crushed
¼ cup (2 fl oz or 60 ml) olive oil
1 small dried red chili pepper

Put the red pepper onto a broiling pan and roast, turning frequently, until blackened all over. Put the pepper into a paper bag and fold the bag closed. Let stand for 10 minutes, then remove from the bag. Peel and seed the pepper and cut it into ¼-inch (1 cm) strips. Set aside.

Cook the broccoli in a large pot of boiling water until just tender, about 5 to 7 minutes. Drain well and rinse under cold running water. Drain well again and gently pad dry. Set aside.

Heat the oil, garlic and chili pepper together in a skillet over high heat until bubbles form around the garlic. Lower the heat to moderately low and cook, stirring constantly, until the garlic and chili pepper are light brown. Strain the mixture through a fine sieve into a bowl. Discard the garlic remaining in the sieve and the chili pepper. Let the strained oil cool slightly and season with salt.

Generously brush the broccoli spears and roasted red pepper strips with the garlic-flavored oil. Arrange on a serving platter and serve.

serves 6

■ Brussels Sprouts with Hazelnuts

¼ cup (60 grams) hazelnuts
6 tablespoons (90 grams) softened sweet butter
1 tablespoon finely chopped shallot
1¼ pounds (550 grams) fresh Brussels sprouts
salt to taste, if desired

Put the hazelnuts into a shallow baking dish. Toast in the oven until lightly browned, about 5 to 10 minutes. Remove the hazelnuts from the oven and put them onto a clean kitchen towel. Rub the nuts in the towel to remove the skins.

Coarsely chop 8 of the hazelnuts. Set aside. Put the remaining hazelnuts into the container of a food processor or blender and process until finely ground.

Heat 1 tablespoon (15 grams) of the butter in a skillet over moderate heat. When the foam subsides, add the shallots. Lower the heat and sauté until the shallots are soft but not browned, about 5 minutes. Remove the skillet from the heat and let the shallots cool to room temperature.

In a bowl combine the remaining butter, ground hazelnuts and cooled shallots. Mix until well blended. Cover the bowl and refrigerate until needed.

Cook the Brussels sprouts in a large saucepan of lightly salted boiling water until tender, about 3 to 5 minutes. The cooking time will depend on the size of the sprouts. Drain well in a colander.

In a saucepan over very low heat, melt the hazelnut butter. Break the butter up with a spoon and stir. The butter will melt into a creamy mass. Do not let it get too hot or it will become oily. Add the Brussels sprouts to the skillet and toss well to coat with the butter.

Put the Brussels sprouts into a serving bowl. Sprinkle with the reserved chopped nuts and serve at once.

serves 4 to 6

■ Shredded Carrots and Squash

2 medium-sized carrots, peeled
1 medium-sized zucchini (courgette)
1 medium-sized yellow squash
3 tablespoons (45 grams) sweet butter
3 shallots, finely chopped
salt to taste, if desired
freshly ground black pepper to taste

Shred the carrots, zucchini and yellow squash, using the shredding blade of a food processor or the coarse side of a hand grater. Put the shredded vegetables into a large mixing bowl and set aside.

Melt the butter in a large skillet over high heat. When the foam subsides, add the shallots and sauté until wilted, about 30 seconds. Stir often.

Add the shredded vegetables to the skillet. Sauté, tossing frequently, until just tender, about 4 minutes. Season with salt and pepper and serve hot.

serves 4

■ Baby Carrots with Parsley and Butter

1 pound (450 grams) baby carrots, peeled and trimmed
2 tablespoons (30 grams) sweet butter
2 teaspoons chopped fresh parsley

Cook the carrots in boiling water to cover until just tender, about 4 to 6 minutes. Drain well.

Melt the butter in a saucepan over moderate heat. Add the parsley and stir. Add the carrots and toss them in the butter and parsley until they are coated, about 1 to 2 minutes. Season with salt and pepper and serve.

serves 4

■ Roasted Corn (Sweet Corn) with Herb Butter

¾ cup (180 grams) softened sweet butter
1½ tablespoons finely chopped fresh parsley
1½ tablespoons finely chopped fresh chives
1½ tablespoons finely chopped scallions (green onions), white parts only
1½ teaspoons fresh lemon juice
salt to taste, if desired
½ teaspoon Tabasco sauce
Worcestershire sauce to taste
freshly ground black pepper to taste
8 ears fresh corn (sweet corn)

Put the butter, parsley, chives, scallions, lemon juice, salt, Tabasco sauce, Worcestershire sauce and pepper into a bowl. Mix until well blended. Cover the bowl and refrigerate for 1 to 2 hours.

Prepare coals, the broiler or the cooker for roasting. Remove the butter from the refrigerator.

Pull back the corn husks from the ears, but do not detach them. Remove the corn silks from the ears. Spread each ear of corn with 1 tablespoon (15 grams) of the herb butter. Carefully wrap the husks back around the ears and wrap each ear in aluminum foil.

Roast the corn over hot coals or in a broiler or cooker 4 inches (10 cm) from the heat source until tender, about 30 minutes. Turn the ears frequently.

When done, remove the aluminum foil. Pull off the husks and brush the corn with additional butter. Serve at once.

serves 4

■ Corn and Potato Salad with Basil Dressing

4 ears fresh corn (sweet corn)
1½ pounds (675 grams) new potatoes
1 tablespoon white wine vinegar
½ medium-sized red onion, finely chopped
1 cup (225 grams) quartered cherry tomatoes
salt to taste, if desired
freshly ground black pepper to taste
Basil Dressing:
4 tablespoons white wine vinegar
1 cup (225 grams) chopped fresh basil leaves
1 garlic clove, minced
4 tablespoons white wine vinegar
½ cup (4 fl oz or 120 ml) olive oil

Shuck the corn and put the ears into a large saucepan. Add enough cold water to cover and bring to the boil. When the water is at a rapid boil, remove the saucepan from the heat and drain the corn well. Let the corn cool until it can be handled easily.

Using a sharp knife, remove the corn kernels from the cobs. With the back of a spoon, scrape the cobs to remove the remaining parts of the kernels. Place the corn into a large mixing bowl.

Quarter the new potatoes lengthwise and cut them crosswise into ¾-inch (2 cm)

slices. Put the potato slices into a steamer over boiling water. Cover and steam until the potatoes are just tender, about 8 minutes. Do not overcook.

Add the potatoes to the corn. Add 1 tablespoon of vinegar and salt to taste. Toss gently.

Combine the basil, garlic and 4 tablespoons vinegar in the container of a food processor or blender. Process until well blended. Add the olive oil and continue to process until the dressing is smooth and well blended. Pour the dressing over the corn and potato mixture.

Add the onion, tomatoes, salt and pepper and toss well. Serve the salad at room temperature.

serves 4 to 6

■ Green Beans with Basil

1 large garlic clove, thinly sliced
14 fresh basil leaves
salt to taste, if desired
4 tablespoons white wine vinegar
¼ cup (2 fl oz or 60 ml) olive oil
¼ cup (2 fl oz or 60 ml) walnut oil
1½ pounds (675 grams) small green beans (French beans)
2 scallions (green onions), white parts only, very thinly sliced

Put the garlic, basil, salt and pepper into the container of a food processor or blender. Process until the mixture is a smooth paste. Put the mixture into a small mixing bowl. In a slow, steady stream, whisk in the olive oil and walnut oil. Set aside.

Cook the green beans (French beans) in a steamer over boiling water until tender, about 8 to 10 minutes. Drain and rinse under cold running water. Drain well again.

Put the beans into a serving bowl. Pour the basil dressing over the beans and toss until well coated. Add the scallions and toss well again.

Let the beans stand at room temperature until they are cool. Toss well several times as the beans cool and immediately before serving.

serves 6

■ Green Beans and Carrots with Hot Onion Dressing

*12 ounces (340 grams) fresh green beans
   (French beans)*
2 large carrots, peeled and julienned
1 onion, coarsely chopped
2 tablespoons vegetable oil
2 tablespoons red wine vinegar
*1 tablespoon chopped fresh dill or ¼ teaspoon
   dried dill*
salt to taste, if desired
freshly ground black pepper to taste

Cook the green beans (French beans) and carrots in boiling water to cover until tender but still crisp, about 10 minutes. Drain well and put into a serving bowl.

Heat the vegetable oil in a saucepan. Add the onion and cook, stirring often, until tender, about 5 minutes. Add the vinegar, dill, salt and pepper. Stir well.

Pour the hot dressing over the beans. Toss well and serve at once.

serves 4

■ Mushrooms Sautéed in Sherry

2 tablespoons (30 grams) sweet butter
2 tablespoons olive oil
*¾ pound (340 grams) fresh mushrooms,
   thickly sliced*
½ cup (120 grams) coarsely chopped onions
1 cup (8 fl oz or 240 ml) dry sherry
salt to taste, if desired
freshly ground black pepper to taste
1 tablespoon finely chopped parsley

Melt the butter with 1 tablespoon olive oil in a large skillet over moderately high heat. Add the mushrooms and sauté, stir-

ring often, until softened, about 2 minutes. Using a slotted spoon, remove the mushrooms from the skillet and reserve.

Lower the heat to moderately low and add the remaining olive oil to the skillet. Add the onions and cook until soft but not brown, about 5 minutes. Add the sherry and stir. Raise the heat to high and bring the mixture to a boil. Continue to boil until reduced by half, about 5 to 6 minutes.

Lower the heat again to moderately low. Add the reserved mushrooms to the skillet and season with salt and pepper. Simmer the mushrooms gently for 5 minutes. Add the parsley and stir.

Transfer the mushrooms to a serving bowl and serve at once.

serves 4 to 6

■ Steamed New Potatoes with Mint

2 pounds (900 grams) new potatoes
*1 or more tablespoons finely chopped fresh
   mint leaves*
4 tablespoons (60 grams) sweet butter, melted

Rinse the potatoes well in cold water and dry thoroughly. Cut the potatoes into ¼-inch (1 cm) slices.

Put the potatoes into a steamer and steam, partially covered, until just tender, about 6 to 10 minutes. Carefully transfer the potatoes to a serving dish.

Sprinkle the potatoes with the mint and salt. Drizzle the melted butter over the potatoes and serve at once.

serves 6

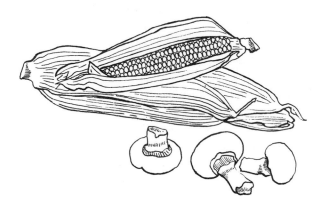

Potato Salad with Vermouth

1¼ pounds (550 grams) potatoes
salt to taste, if desired
freshly ground black pepper to taste
1½ tablespoons dry vermouth or dry white wine
¼ cup (2 fl oz or 60 ml) olive oil
¼ cup (60 grams) chopped fresh parsley

Wash the potatoes and put them in a large saucepan with enough water to cover. Bring to the boil, reduce the heat, and cook until tender, about 20 minutes. Do not overcook. Drain well and let the potatoes cool.

Preheat the oven to 200°F (95°C).

When the potatoes are cool enough to handle easily, peel them and cut them into ¼-inch (1 cm) slices. Put the slices into an ovenproof serving dish or casserole dish. Season the slices with salt and pepper. Add the vermouth or white wine and the olive oil and toss gently but well. Cover the bowl or dish with aluminum foil and bake until heated through, about 10 to 15 minutes.

Remove the dish or casserole from the oven. Remove the foil, sprinkle the potatoes with the parsley, and toss well. Serve salad warm or at room temperature.

serves 4

New Potatoes with Lemon Sauce

2 pounds (900 grams) small red new potatoes, peeled
2 tablespoons olive oil
2 garlic cloves, finely chopped
2 cups (16 fl oz or 480 ml) chicken broth
2 tablespoons fresh lemon juice
salt to taste, if desired
freshly ground black pepper to taste
½ cup (120 grams) finely chopped scallions (green onions)

Rinse the peeled potatoes in cold water and dry well.

Heat the olive oil in a large skillet over moderately high heat. Add the potatoes and cook for 2 minutes, turning often to coat the potatoes with the olive oil. Reduce the heat to low and add the garlic, chicken broth, lemon juice, salt and pepper. Cover the skillet securely and simmer gently until the potatoes are tender, about 25 minutes. Check the potatoes occasionally as they cook to be sure they are not sticking to the skillet.

Transfer the potatoes to a serving dish with a slotted spoon. Cover and keep warm.

Raise the heat under the skillet and boil the cooking liquid, uncovered, until it is reduced and slightly thicker. Add the scallions and cook for 2 minutes longer.

Pour the sauce over the potatoes and serve.

serves 6

Spaghetti Squash with Parmesan Cheese

1 large spaghetti squash
¼ cup (60 grams) sweet butter
2 garlic cloves, minced
salt to taste, if desired
freshly ground black pepper to taste
½ cup (120 grams) freshly grated Parmesan cheese

Preheat the oven to 350°F (180°C).

Put the wholel squash on a baking sheet and bake until the skin begins to give way and can be easily pierced with a fork, about 1 hour. Remove the squash from the oven.

When cool enough to handle, cut the squash in half lengthwise and remove the seeds. Using a fork, fluff up the fibrous strands inside the squash until they resemble strands of spaghetti. Scrape the strands from the squash halves.

Put the squash strands into a baking or

casserole dish. Add the butter, garlic, salt, pepper and Parmesan cheese and toss well. Bake until heated through, about 5 to 10 minutes. Serve hot.

serves 4

■ Red Cabbage Rolls with Vegetable Filling

1 medium-sized head red cabbage
1 cup (8 fl oz or 240 ml) red wine vinegar
2 tablespoons cassis or blackberry liqueur
4 ounces (120 grams) softened cream cheese
¼ cup (2 fl oz or 60 ml) olive oil
2 tablespoons fresh lemon juice
2 tablespoons heavy cream (single cream)
coarse salt to taste, if desired
freshly ground black pepper to taste
2 small zucchini (courgettes), julienned
2 small yellow squash, julienned
2 medium-sized carrots, peeled and julienned
1 large sweet red pepper, julienned
1 celery stalk, julienned

Core the cabbage but leave the head whole. Remove the tough outer leaves.

Bring the water to a boil in a large pot. Add the cabbage, cored side down. Using two forks, gently pull 8 leaves away from the head. Drain the cabbage. Reserve the rest of the head for another use.

Fill the same large pot with water to the depth of 1 inch (2.5 cm). Add the red wine vinegar and cassis and bring the mixture to a boil. Add 4 of the cabbage leaves and simmer over low heat until the leaves are slightly softer, about 1 minute. Remove the leaves and drain well. Cook the remaining leaves in the same way.

Let the leaves cool and then trim off any tough ribs. Gently pat the leaves dry.

In a large bowl combine the cream cheese, olive oil, lemon juice and cream. Season with salt and pepper and mix until well blended.

Add the julienned vegetables to the cream cheese mixture. Toss until the vegetables are well coated. Let the mixture

stand at room temperature for 20 minutes. Drain off any liquid that accumulates in the bowl.

Spread the cabbage leaves flat. Spoon about ½ cup (120 grams) of the vegetable mixture onto each cabbage leaf. Roll the leaves tightly and secure them closed with wooden toothpicks. Put the rolls on a plate, cover and refrigerate for 2 hours.

To serve, drain off any liquid that accumulates on the plate. Put the cabbage rolls on a serving platter and serve cold.

serves 8

■ Sautéed Sweet Potatoes with Shallots

2 pounds (900 grams) sweet potatoes
7 tablespoons (105 grams) sweet butter
8 shallots, quartered
¾ cup (6 fl oz or 180 ml) chicken broth
salt to taste, if desired
freshly ground black pepper to taste

Peel the sweet potatoes and cut them into ¼-inch (1 cm) slices. Cut each slice into quarters.

Melt 3 tablespoons (45 grams) of the butter in a skillet over moderately high heat. Add half the sweet potatoes and sauté until they are light brown, about 8 to 10 minutes. Remove the sweet potatoes from the skillet and put them in a bowl. Add 3 tablespoons (45 grams) more butter to the skillet and cook the remaining sweet potatoes as above.

Melt the remaining tablespoon (15 grams) of the butter in the skillet over moderate heat. Add the shallots and sauté until light brown, about 6 to 8 minutes. Stir in the chicken broth and simmer the mixture, stirring often, until the shallots are cooked and glazed, about 5 minutes.

Raise the heat to moderately high and return the sweet potatoes to the skillet. Cook until they are golden brown and heated through, about 5 minutes. Use a spatula to turn the potatoes. Be sure they heat and brown evenly.

Remove the sweet potato mixture from the skillet and put into a serving dish. Serve at once.

serves 4 to 6

■ Sautéed Watercress

3 bunches watercress
salt to taste, if desired
freshly ground black pepper to taste
2½ tablespoons (40 grams) sweet butter
2 tablespoons water

Discard any tough stems and blemished leaves from the watercress. Rinse thoroughly under cold running water and drain well. Gently pat dry. Put the watercress into a bowl and season with salt and pepper.

Put a large skillet over high heat and heat until very hot. Add the butter and water. Heat the mixture, shaking the pan often, until the butter melts and combines with the water.

Add the watercress to the skillet. Toss until the leaves are just wilted and completely coated with butter, about 45 to 50 seconds. Remove the skillet from the heat. Transfer the watercress to a serving dish and serve immediately.

serves 4

■ Sautéed Zucchini (Courgettes) with Fresh Herbs

1½ pounds (675 grams) zucchini
 (courgettes), thinly sliced
4 tablespoons olive oil
salt to taste, if desired
freshly ground black pepper to taste
2 tablespoons (30 grams) sweet butter
2 teaspoons finely chopped garlic
1 tablespoon finely chopped fresh parsley
1 tablespoon finely chopped fresh dill
1 tablespoon finely chopped fresh chives
1 tablespoon finely chopped fresh basil
1 teaspoon finely chopped fresh tarragon

Heat the olive oil in a skillet over high heat until very hot. Add the zucchini (courgettes) slices and cook, stirring frequently, until tender, about 5 minutes. Season with salt and pepper, stir again, and remove from the skillet with a slotted spoon. Drain the zucchini (courgettes) in a colander or sieve.

Melt the butter in the skillet. Return the drained zucchini (courgettes) to the skillet and add the garlic, parsley, chives, dill, basil and tarragon. Toss well, transfer to a serving dish, and serve hot.

serves 6

Breads

If bread is the staff of life, then we are leaning on a precarious walking stick. Most of the bread available in the markets today is poor stuff, factory manufactured in uniform loaves, wonderful for absorbing spreads and absolutely devoid of any recognizable flavor. It is truly produced for the lowest common denominator; though filling, it has nothing else to recommend it.

Bread-making is one of the more satisfying kitchen vocations. The mixing, kneading, rising and baking is in itself much fun, but the aroma of the final golden loaves emerging from the oven is enough to make the most hardened kitchen cynic sniff deeply and smile. Bread-making need not be time-consuming. A number of quick rolls, breads, muffins and scones allow wide latitude in what the home baker can easily produce.

More to the point, these home-baked breads will be made from known ingredients…butter, whole-grain flour, yeast, eggs and salt, with no artificial stabilizers, preservatives and other potentially harmful chemicals. It will be fresh and crusty. It will taste out of this world. In fact, it can often become the highlight of a meal.

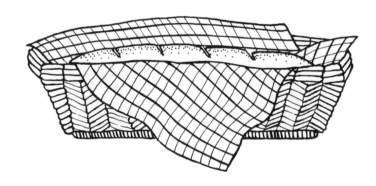

■ Spiral Bread

2 tablespoons (30 grams) softened sweet
    butter
2 shallots, finely chopped
1 cup (225 grams) finely chopped fresh
    parsley
1 garlic clove, crushed
2 teaspoons finely chopped fresh thyme or 1
    teaspoon crumbled dried thyme
15 finely chopped basil leaves or 1 tablespoon
    crumbled dried basil
1 egg, beaten
salt to taste, if desired
cayenne pepper to taste
freshly ground black pepper to taste
Tabasco sauce to taste
½ cup (4 fl oz or 120 ml) very warm water
1 package (7 grams) active dry yeast
½ cup (4 fl oz or 120 ml) scalded milk
1 tablespoon (15 grams) sugar
1 tablespoon (15 grams) salt
4 tablespoons (60 grams) sweet butter
3 to 4 cups (420 to 550 grams) flour (plain
    flour)
1 egg, beaten

Melt the 2 tablespoons (30 grams) softened butter in a large skillet. Add the shallots, parsley, garlic, thyme and basil. Sauté over medium heat, stirring often, for 10 minutes. Put the mixture into a bowl.

Add the egg, salt, cayenne pepper, black pepper and Tabasco sauce to the bowl. Stir to mix well. Set the filling aside until needed.

Put the warm water into a large bowl and add the yeast. Stir to dissolve. Let the mixture stand at room temperature for 10 minutes.

Add the milk, sugar, salt and 4 tablespoons (60 grams) butter to the yeast. Stir until well blended. Add 3 cups (420 grams) of the flour and mix well. Add more flour as needed to form a solid dough. Let the dough rest in the bowl for 10 minutes.

Turn the dough onto a lightly floured surface and knead for 12 to 15 minutes. Put the kneaded dough into a lightly buttered bowl and turn it to coat the dough with the butter. Cover the bowl with a clean kitchen towel and let it rise in a warm place until it is doubled in size, about 1 hour.

Punch the dough down and let it rest in the bowl for 12 to 15 minutes.

Turn the dough onto a lightly floured surface and roll it out into a rectangle that is ¼-inch (1 cm) thick and 10 inches (25 cm) long by 6 inches (15 cm) wide. Brush the surface of the dough with half the beaten egg. Spread the filling over the dough, leaving a thin border all around. Carefully roll the dough up and seal the edges.

Put the dough into a well-greased 9 × 5 × 3-inch (23 × 13 × 8 cm) loaf pan. Brush the top of the loaf with the remaining beaten egg. Let the loaf rise in a warm spot for 1 hour.

Preheat the oven to 375°F (190°C).

Bake the bread until the top is golden brown, about 50 to 60 minutes. Remove from the oven and cool for 15 minutes on a wire rack. Carefully remove the loaf from the pan and cool it completely on the rack.

makes 1 loaf

■ Carrot Coconut Bread

2 cups (280 grams) flour (plain flour)
1¼ cups (280 grams) sugar
2 teaspoons ground cinnamon
2 teaspoons baking soda
½ teaspoon salt
½ cup (120 grams) grated unsweetened
    coconut
½ cup (120 grams) currants
½ cups (120 grams) coarsely chopped pecans
    or filberts
2 cups (450 grams) coarsely grated carrot
1 cup (8 fl oz or 240 ml) vegetable oil
2 eggs
2 teaspoons pure vanilla extract

Preheat the oven to 350°F (180°C). Generously butter an 8 × 4 × 2½-inch (20 × 10 × 7 cm) loaf pan.

Combine the flour, sugar, cinnamon, baking soda and salt together in a large mixing bowl. Add the coconut, currants, and nuts. Mix until well blended.

Add the grated carrots, oil, eggs and vanilla extract. Mix well, using a wooden spoon, until all the ingredients are thoroughly combined.

Pour the batter into the prepared pan. Bake until the bread shrinks slightly from the sides of the pan and a cake tester inserted into the center of the bread comes out clean, about 30 to 40 minutes.

Remove the pan from the oven and put it on a wire rack. Cool the bread in the pan for 10 minutes. Turn the loaf out onto the rack and cool completely. This loaf slices best if it is aged for a day.

makes 1 loaf

■ Onion and Parsley Bread

4 tablespoons (60 grams) sweet butter
1 cup (225 grams) coarsely chopped onion
½ cup (4 fl oz or 120 ml) very warm water
2 packages (14 grams) active dry yeast
4 tablespoons (60 grams) light brown sugar
1½ cups (12 fl oz or 360 ml) milk
1 teaspoon salt
1 egg, beaten
5 cups (700 grams) sifted flour (plain flour)
⅓ cup (75 grams) finely chopped parsley
2 tablespoons (30 grams) butter, melted

Generously butter an 8-cup (3½ pints or 2 litre) soufflé or casserole dish. Set aside.

Melt the butter in a skillet. Add the onion and sauté over moderate heat until lightly browned, about 5 to 8 minutes. Remove from the heat and set aside.

Put the water into a small bowl. Add the yeast and 2 tablespoons (30 grams) of the brown sugar and stir until dissolved. Let stand at room temperature for 10 minutes. The mixture will be bubbly.

Heat the milk in a saucepan over moderate heat until bubbles start to form. Add the salt and the remaining brown sugar to the saucepan. Stir to dissolve. Remove the saucepan from the heat and cool to room temperature. Pour the mixture into a large bowl.

Add the yeast mixture, onions, egg and flour to the milk mixture. Mix with a wooden spoon or electric mixer until very well blended, about 3 to 4 minutes. Add the parsley and stir.

Turn the dough into the prepared dish. Cover with a sheet of buttered waxed paper and then a clean kitchen towel. Put the dough in a warm place and let rise until doubled in size, about 45 minutes.

Preheat the oven to 375°F (190°C).

Bake the bread until it sounds hollow when tapped, about 35 to 40 minutes. Remove from the oven and carefully turn the bread out onto a wire rack. Brush the top of the loaf with melted butter and serve warm.

makes 1 round loaf

■ Zucchini (Courgette) Rolls

⅔ cup (150 grams) coarsely grated zucchini (courgette)
3½ cups (500 grams) flour (plain flour)
½ teaspoon salt
2 tablespoons vegetable oil
½ cup (4 fl oz or 120 ml) warm water
1 teaspoon flour (plain flour)
2 teaspoons honey
1 package (7 grams) active dry yeast
1 cup (8 fl oz or 240 ml) warm milk

Drain the grated zucchini (courgette) in a colander for 30 minutes.

In a large bowl combine the flour, salt, grated zucchini (courgette) and oil.

In a small bowl combine the warm water, 1 teaspoon flour, honey and yeast. Stir until the ingredients are dissolved. Add the warm milk and stir again. Quickly pour the mixture into the zucchini (courgette) mixture in the large bowl. Stir until well blended.

Turn the dough out onto a lightly floured surface and knead until the dough is soft and firm, about 10 minutes. Add more flour as needed.

Put the kneaded dough into a generously buttered bowl. Turn the dough to coat it with the butter. Cover with a clean towel and let the dough rise in a warm place until it is doubled in size, about 50 to 60 minutes.

Turn the dough out onto a lightly floured surface and knead for 5 minutes. Shape the dough into 12 to 16 small rolls. Put the rolls into well-greased muffin tins. Cover with a clean towel and let rise in a warm place for 30 minutes.

Preheat the oven to 400°F (200°C).

Put the rolls into the oven and reduce the heat to 375°F (190°C). Bake until the rolls are golden brown, about 15 to 20 minutes.

Remove the rolls from the oven, turn out of the muffin tins and serve warm.

makes 12 to 16 rolls

■ Ginger Pecan Muffins

1 cup (150 grams) pecans or filberts
1 cup (150 grams) flour (plain flour)
1 teaspoon salt
1 teaspoon baking powder
½ teaspoon baking soda
¾ teaspoon ground cinnamon
¾ teaspoon ground ginger
½ teaspoon nutmeg
¾ cup (100 grams) packed light brown sugar
1 egg, lightly beaten
1 cup (8 fl oz or 240 ml) buttermilk
⅓ cup (75 grams) butter, melted

Preheat the oven to 400°F (200°C).

Put the nuts in a shallow dish or on a baking sheet. Toast them in the oven until golden, about 5 minutes. Let the nuts cool, then chop them coarsely and set aside.

Combine the flour, salt, baking powder, baking soda, cinnamon, ginger and nutmeg in a large bowl. Mix well. Add the whole wheat flour, sugar and chopped nuts. Mix well.

Add the buttermilk and melted butter to the beaten egg in a bowl. Beat until well combined. Pour into the flour mixture and stir only until the mixtures are just combined; muffin batter should be lumpy.

Divide the batter among 12 buttered muffin tins. Bake the muffins until a cake tester inserted into the center of a muffin comes out clean, about 25 minutes.

Remove the muffins from the oven and cool in the tin on a wire rack for 5 minutes. Turn the muffins out of the tin onto a wire rack and cool slightly before serving.

makes 12 muffins

■ Apricot and Pecan Loaf

1½ cups (360 grams) sifted flour (plain
  flour)
2 teaspoons baking powder
½ teaspoon salt
¼ teaspoon baking soda
½ cup (120 grams) sugar
½ cup (120 grams) coarsely chopped dried
  apricots
½ cup (120 grams) coarsely chopped pecans
  or filberts
1 teaspoon grated orange rind
1 egg, lightly beaten
¾ cup (6 fl oz or 180 ml) milk
¼ cup (2 fl oz or 80 ml) vegetable oil

Preheat the oven to 350°F (180°C). Generously butter a 9 × 5 × 3-inch (23 × 13 ×
8 cm) loaf pan. Set aside.

Sift the flour together with the baking
powder, salt and baking soda. Add the
sugar, apricots and nuts and mix well.

Add the orange rind, egg, milk and
vegetable oil. Stir until the mixture is well
blended. Pour the batter into the prepared
pan.

Bake until a cake tester inserted into the
center of the bread comes out clean, about
45 to 50 minutes. Remove from the oven
and cool in the pan for 10 minutes. Carefully turn the loaf out from the pan and
cool thoroughly on a wire rack.

makes 1 loaf

■ Nutted Banana Bread

2½ cup (350 grams) flour (plain flour)
2 teaspoons baking powder
½ teaspoon baking soda
½ teaspoon salt
½ cup (120 grams) softened sweet butter
1 cup (225 grams) sugar
2 eggs
3 very ripe bananas, mashed with ½
  teaspoon water
1 teaspoon pure vanilla extract
½ cup (120 grams) coarsely chopped walnuts

Preheat the oven to 375°F (190°C). Generously butter a 9 × 5 × 3-inch (23 × 13 ×
8 cm) loaf pan. Set aside.

Sift the flour together with the baking
powder, baking soda and salt onto a large
sheet of waxed paper. Set aside.

Cream the butter and sugar together in
a large mixing bowl. Add the eggs, one at
a time, beating well after each addition.
Add the mashed bananas and the vanilla
extract. Stir until well mixed.

Stir in the sifted flour mixture. Mix until
well combined. Add the walnuts and stir.

Turn the batter into the prepared pan
and bake until a cake tester inserted into
the center of the bread comes out clean,
about 35 minutes. Carefully turn out the
loaf from the pan and cool completely on
a wire rack.

makes 1 loaf

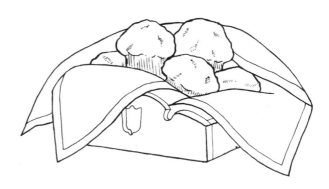

■ Whole-Kernel Corn Muffins

1 cup (225 grams) fresh corn (sweet corn; about 2 to 3 ears)
1 cup (150 grams) flour (plain flour)
½ cup (120 grams) yellow cornmeal
½ cup (120 grams) sugar
1 tablespoon baking powder
½ teaspoon salt
2 eggs, beaten
½ cup (4 fl oz or 120 ml) milk
½ cup (120 grams) butter, melted

Preheat the oven to 400°F (200°C).

Using a small, sharp knife, cut the corn kernels from the cobs. Scrape the cobs with the side of a spoon to remove all the kernel. Set the kernels aside.

Combine the flour, cornmeal, sugar, baking powder and salt together in a large bowl. Mix well. Add the corn kernels and stir until they are well coated.

Add the milk and melted butter to the beaten eggs in a bowl. Mix until well blended. Pour into the flour mixture and stir only until the mixtures are just combined; muffin batter should be lumpy.

Divide the batter among 12 buttered muffin tins. Bake the muffins until a cake tester inserted into the center of a muffin comes out clean, about 15 to 20 minutes.

Remove the muffins from the oven and cool in the tin on a wire rack for 5 minutes. Turn the muffins out of the tin onto a wire rack and cool slightly before serving.

makes 12 muffins

■ Zucchini (Courgette) and Lemon Muffins

2 cups (280 grams) flour (plain flour)
½ cup (120 grams) sugar
1 tablespoon baking powder
1 teaspoon salt
1 teaspoon grated lemon rind
½ teaspoon grated nutmeg
½ cup (120 grams) coarsely chopped walnuts
¼ cup (60 grams) dark raisins
¼ cup (60 grams) golden raisins
2 eggs, beaten
½ cup (4 fl oz or 120 ml) milk
⅓ cup (3 fl oz or 80 ml) milk
1 cup (225 grams) coarsely grated zucchini (courgette)

Preheat the oven to 400°F (200°C).

Combine the flour, sugar, baking powder, salt, lemon rind and nutmeg in a large bowl. Add the raisins and walnuts and stir well.

Add the milk and oil to the beaten eggs in a bowl. Beat until well blended. Pour the mixture into the bowl with the flour mixture; do not stir. Add the grated zucchini. Stir only until the ingredients are just combined; muffin batter should be lumpy.

Divide the batter among 12 buttered muffin tins. Bake the muffins until a cake tester inserted into the center of a muffin comes out clean, about 15 to 20 minutes.

Remove the muffins from the oven and cool in the tin on a wire rack for 5 minutes. Turn the muffins out of the tin onto a wire rack and cool completely before serving.

makes 12 muffins

Desserts

Rich cakes, cream-filled pastries and other multicolored concoctions certainly have their place. But after a fairly filling and elaborate meal, eating one can be like pouring molten lead upon the bulging stomach. Other dessert possibilities exist, and ones more suited to making leaving the table something other than a test of one's strength and athletic endurance.

After a large dinner, the obvious solution to the dessert question is perfectly ripe fresh fruit, served iced in a bowl. Supply small sharp knifes and plates for each guest, add perhaps a good cheese or two and some water biscuits, and your dessert problem is solved. A homemade ice or sorbet can be equally good.

Combinations of fruits with liqueurs, on light cushions of pastry with a touch of cream, can be most elegant endings to a meal, as can mousses, flans, creams and souf-flés. Whatever it is must be very fresh and very simply presented.

Do not feel compelled to dress up everything with globs of whipped cream, dots of jellies or bits of preserved or crystalized fruits. Desserts are at their best when they come unadorned, with only the beauty of the ingredients shining through.

The same goes for cakes and pastries. Don't get carried away with decoration. Rather, use the best ingredients to make a simple pudding or tart, a chocolate cake with no icing but just the slightest dusting of powdered sugar, a fruit bread or a simple crêpe with fruit. All can offer the satisfaction of the gaudiest multilayered extravaganza with a good bit more discretion.

Above all, your guests should leave the table with at least a millimeter of capacity left. After all, they might want a mint later on.

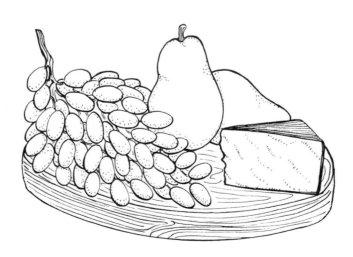

■ Poached Pears with Raspberry Syrup

20 ounces (560 grams) thawed frozen
  raspberries, with juice
½ cup (120 grams) crème de cassis or
  blackberry-flavored liqueur
8 firm ripe pears
finely chopped pistachio nuts

Purée the raspberries in a blender or food processor until smooth. Strain the purée through a fine sieve into a large mixing bowl. Discard any solids remaining in the sieve. Add the crème de cassis to the purée and stir. Set aside.

Peel the pears. Using a sharp knife or corer, core the pears from the bottom, leaving the tops and stems intact. Cut off a thin slice from the bottom of each half. Arrange the pears, standing upright, in a large saucepan.

Pour the raspberry and crème de cassis mixture over the pears. Bring the liquid to a gentle boil. Cover and simmer until the pears are tender, about 8 to 10 minutes. Remove the pears from the saucepan and cool to room temperature, then chill for at least 2 hours.

Transfer the cooking liquid to a smaller saucepan. Bring the liquid to a boil. Continue to boil until the liquid is reduced to a thick syrup, about 10 to 12 minutes. Remove the saucepan from the heat and let the syrup cool.

To serve, lightly coat individual serving plates with some syrup. Arrange the pears on the plates and drizzle the remaining syrup evenly over them. Sprinkle with the chopped pistachios and serve.

■ Summer Fruits with Rum Sauce

2 sweet apples
4 ripe peaches
2 tablespoons fresh lemon juice
1 ripe cantaloupe
2 cups (450 grams) hulled ripe strawberries
1 cup (225 grams) ripe blueberries
⅓ cup (3 fl oz or 80 ml) honey
2 tablespoons dark rum
3 tablespoons (45 grams) sweet butter
fresh mint leaves for garnish

Peel, core and thinly slice the apples. Peel and thinly slice the peaches. Toss the apple and peach slices in the lemon juice. Using a melon baller, scoop balls out of the cantaloupe.

In a large bowl, combine the apples, peaches, cantaloupe balls, strawberries and blueberries. Toss gently.

Combine the honey, rum and butter in a saucepan. Cook over low heat, stirring constantly, until the butter is melted.

Divide the fruit mixture evenly among individual serving bowls. Spoon the sauce over the fruit and garnish each bowl with fresh mint leaves. Serve at once.

serves 8

■ Tangy Lemon Sorbet

1¾ cup (400 grams) superfine sugar (icing
  sugar)
1 cup (8 fl oz or 240 ml) plus 2 tablespoons
  water
1⅓ cups (11 fl oz or 320 ml) strained fresh
  lemon juice
1⅓ cups (11 fl oz or 320 ml) noncarbonated
  mineral water
1 egg white

Combine the sugar and water together in a saucepan. Cook over low heat, stirring occasionally, until the sugar dissolves. Raise the heat and bring the mixture to a boil. Remove from the heat and cool to room temperature. Refrigerate until cold, about 1 hour.

Remove the syrup from the refrigerator and add the lemon juice and mineral water. Stir until well blended.

Transfer the syrup mixture to an electric ice-cream maker and process according to the manufacturer's instructions only until the mixture begins to thicken and freeze.

Remove 3 tablespoons of the sorbet from the ice-cream maker and put them into a small bowl. Add the egg white and beat with a wire whisk until foamy and thick, about 2 minutes.

Return the egg-white mixture to the sorbet still in the ice-cream maker and continue to process until the sorbet reaches the desired consistency.

Transfer the sorbet to a large bowl. Cover tightly and freeze until firm, about 3 hours.

To serve, scoop the sorbet into chilled individual serving dishes and serve at once.

makes 4 cups (900 grams)

■ Sparkling Kiwi Sorbet

as served at Wheeler's Restaurant, Auckland, New Zealand

½ cup (120 grams) sugar
½ cup (4 fl oz or 120 ml) water
8 kiwis, peeled and cubed
1 cup (8 fl oz or 240 ml) dry champagne
1 teaspoon or more fresh lemon juice
1 egg white, lightly beaten

Combine the sugar and water together in a saucepan. Cook, stirring often, over moderate heat until the mixture begins to boil. Remove the syrup from the heat and let cool to room temperature.

Purée the kiwi in a food processor or blender until smooth. Strain the purée through a sieve into a large mixing bowl, using the back of a spoon to push the purée through. Discard any solids remaining in the sieve.

Add the cooled syrup and the cham-pagne to the purée. Stir until well blended. Add 1 teaspoon or more lemon juice to taste to the mixture and stir again.

Transfer the mixture to an electric ice-cream maker and process according to the manufacturer's instructions only until the mixture begins to freeze but is still slushy. Add the beaten egg white and continue to process until the sorbet is partially frozen.

Transfer the sorbet from the ice-cream maker to a bowl. Cover tightly and freeze until firm, about 2 to 3 hours.

To serve, scoop the sorbet into chilled individual serving dishes and serve at once. This sorbet should be used when made; it will not keep for more than three days in the freezer.

makes 2½ cups (550 grams)

■ Frozen Campari Mousse

¾ cup (180 grams) plus 1 tablespoon sugar
½ cup (4 fl oz or 120 ml) water
3 egg whites
¼ teaspoon salt
¼ teaspoon cream of tartar
3 tablespoons (45 grams) sugar
¼ cup (2 fl oz or 60 ml) Campari
1 cup (8 fl oz or 240 ml) very cold heavy cream (single cream)
whipped cream for garnish

In a small saucepan combine ¾ cup (180 grams) plus 1 tablespoon sugar with the water. Cook over low heat, stirring occasionally, until the sugar dissolves. Raise the heat and bring the mixture to a boil. Continue to boil the syrup until it forms a soft ball when dropped into cold water or registers 240°F (115°C) on a candy thermometer.

While the syrup cooks, beat the egg whites with the salt and the cream of tartar until they are stiff but not dry. Add the remaining sugar, a little at a time, beating after each addition.

In a slow, steady stream, add the hot syrup to the beaten egg whites. Beat the mixture constantly until it is cool, about 8 to 10 minutes.

Add the Campari to the cooled mixture and beat until well blended.

Beat the very cold heavy cream (single cream) in a chilled bowl until soft peaks form. Fold the cream into the egg white and Campari mixture.

Gently spoon the mixture into 6-ounce (6 fl oz or 180 ml) wineglasses or dessert dishes. Freeze, uncovered, for at least 5 hours.

Top with whipped cream before serving, if desired.

serves 6

■ Chilled Chocolate Almond Loaf

as served at The Peasant, Atlanta, Georgia

12 ounces (340 grams) semisweet or
  bittersweet chocolate
1½ cups (340 grams) sugar
½ cup (4 fl oz or 120 ml) water
1½ cups (340 grams) softened sweet butter
2¾ cups (630 grams) unsweetened Dutch-
  process cocoa powder
3 egg yolks
2 eggs
¼ cup (2 fl oz or 60 ml) amaretto or almond-
  flavored liqueur
2 teaspoons almond extract
2½ cups (550 grams) toasted slivered
  almonds
2 tablespoons unsweetened Dutch-process
  cocoa powder
2 cups (16 fl oz or 480 ml) heavy cream
  (single cream)
whipped cream for garnish

Melt the chocolate in the top of a double boiler over hot but not boiling water. Remove from the heat and let the chocolate cool to room temperature.

In a small saucepan combine the sugar and water. Cook over high heat, stirring occasionally, until the mixture begins to boil. Remove from the heat and let the syrup cool to room temperature.

Lightly butter a 9 × 5 × 3-inch (23 × 138 cm) loaf pan. Line the bottom of the pan with a piece of waxed paper cut to fit. Set aside.

In a large mixing bowl combine the butter and cocoa powder. Beat with an electric mixer until smooth, scraping down the sides of the bowl frequently with a rubber spatula. Add the egg yolks and the whole eggs and beat until well blended.

Add the cooled chocolate and the cooled syrup and beat until well blended. Add the amaretto and almond extract and beat until well blended. Add 2 cups (450 grams) of the almonds and stir.

Transfer the mixture to the prepared pan. Level off the top with a rubber spatula. Cover the pan with plastic wrap and refrigerate overnight.

To serve, run a thin, sharp knife around the sides of the pan. Cover the top of the pan with a plate and invert the pan. Sprinkle the top of the loaf with the remaining 2 tablespoons cocoa. Gently press the remaining almond slivers onto the sides of the loaf.

Let the loaf stand at room temperature for 10 to 15 minutes before slicing. Slice and serve topped with whipped cream, if desired.

serves 12 to 16

■ White Chocolate Ice Cream

1 cup (8 fl oz or 240 ml) water
¾ cup (180 grams) sugar
6 egg yolks
1 tablespoon pure vanilla extract
10 ounces (280 grams) white chocolate,
  melted
2 cups (16 fl oz or 480 ml) heavy cream
  (single cream)

Combine the water and sugar in a small saucepan. Cook over low heat, stirring occasionally, until the sugar dissolves. Raise the heat to moderate and bring the mixture to a boil. Continue to boil the syrup for 5 minutes.

While the syrup boils, combine the egg yolks and vanilla in the large bowl of an electric mixer. Beat at high speed until the mixture is light and fluffy, about 5 to 7 minutes.

Very slowly add the hot syrup to the yolk mixture. Beat constantly until the mixture is thick and completely cooled, about 10 minutes.

Add the melted white chocolate, a little at a time, beating after each addition. Continue to beat for 5 to 7 minutes longer.

Add the cream and stir well. Cover the bowl tightly with aluminum foil and freeze for at least 6 hours or overnight before serving.

makes 4 cups (900 grams)

■ Sliced Lemon Pie

2 lemons
2 cups (480 grams) sugar
4 eggs
1 pastry for 2-crust, 9-inch (23 cm) pie (see below)

Preheat the oven to 450°F (230°C).

Slice the lemons into rounds as thin as possible. Remove the pits and put the slices into a bowl. Add the sugar and mix well. Let stand 2 to 3 hours.

Roll out half the pastry onto a lightly floured surface. Fit the pastry into a 9-inch (23 cm) pie pan. Roll out the remaining pastry for a top crust, cut a slit in it, and set aside.

In a small bowl beat the eggs until foamy. Add the eggs to the bowl with the lemon slices and mix well. Pour the mixture into the prepared pastry crust. Cover with the top crust, fit well, seal, and flute.

Bake the pie for 15 minutes. Reduce the oven temperature to 350°F (180°C) and bake 45 minutes longer. Remove from the oven and serve warm.

makes 1 9-inch (23 cm) pie

■ Fresh Fruit Tart

1 cup (150 grams) flour (plain flour)
1 tablespoon (15 grams) sugar
⅛ teaspoon salt
½ cup (110 grams) softened sweet butter
3 ounces (75 grams) softened cream cheese
½ cup (110 grams) apricot preserves
1 tablespoon amaretto or almond liqueur
4 to 6 medium-sized fresh nectarines
⅓ cup (75 grams) sliced almonds

Sift the flour together with the sugar and salt into a large bowl. Cut in the butter with a pastry blender or two knives until the mixture resembles a coarse meal. Add the cream cheese and mix to form a soft dough. Shape the dough into a ball, wrap in waxed paper, and chill for 2 hours.

Preheat the oven to 400°F (200°C).

Place the almonds in a metal baking pan and toast in the oven until golden, about 5 minutes. Remove from oven and cool.

Roll the pastry out onto a lightly floured surface, using a floured rolling pin. Invert it into a 9-inch (23 cm) metal tart pan, preferably one with a removable bottom. Prick the crust with a fork and line it with aluminum foil. Weight the foil down with a handful of dried beans. Bake the crust for 20 minutes. Remove and discard the beans and foil; continue baking the crust until it is lightly browned, about 8 to 10 minutes longer. Remove from the oven and cool completely.

Brush the bottom of the cooled pastry crust lightly with some of the apricot preserves. Put the remaining preserves and the amaretto liqueur into a saucepan. Heat until the preserves melt. Stir well and set aside to use for the glaze.

Peel, pit, and slice the nectarines. Arrange the slices in slightly overlapping concentric circles in the pastry shell. Brush the slices with the melted glaze. Sprinkle with the toasted almonds. Refrigerate until set, about 3 to 4 hours, before serving.

makes 1 9-inch (23 cm) tart

■ Buttery Pie Pastry

1½ cups (225 grams) flour (plain flour)
2 teaspoons sugar
¼ teaspoon salt
4 tablespoons (60 grams) very cold sweet
  butter, cut into 8 equal pieces
4 tablespoons (60 grams) very cold solid
  vegetable shortening
3 tablespoons ice water

Combine the flour, sugar and salt in a medium-sized bowl. Cut in the butter and shortening, using a pastry blender or two knives, until the mixture resembles a very coarse meal. Sprinkle the ice water over the mixture, a little at a time, while tossing with a fork, until the mixture is moist enough to hold shape (this may take additional ice water). Do not overmix; the mixture should be coarse and crumbly.

Turn the dough out onto an unfloured surface. Gently gather the dough together to form a ball. Add more ice water it it is needed to make the mixture adhere. However, be careful not to add too much water, or the mixture will become moist and sticky.

Wrap the dough tightly in plastic wrap and refrigerate for 3 hours or overnight.

When ready to use, remove the dough from the refrigerator and follow the recipe directions.

For pies needing two crusts, simply double the recipe. Divide the dough in half and wrap each half separately before refrigerating.

makes 1 single-crust 9-inch (23 cm) pie

■ Strawberry Tart

¾ cup (120 grams) flour (plain flour)
⅓ cup (75 grams) ground almonds
3 tablespoons (45 grams) sugar
6 tablespoons (90 grams) sweet butter
1 egg yolk, lightly beaten
¾ cup (160 grams) red currant or strawberry
  jelly
2 pints hulled fresh strawberries

Preheat the oven to 400°F (200°C).

In a mixing bowl combine the flour, almonds, and sugar. Using a pastry blender or two knives, or in a food processor, cut in the butter by tablespoons until the mixture resembles a coarse meal. Add the egg yolk and mix until the crumbs form a dough.

Roll the dough out into a thin sheet. Fit the dough into a 9-inch tart pan with a removable bottom. Line the dough with a piece of aluminum foil and weight down the foil with a handful or dried beans. Bake the shell for 10 minutes. Reduce the oven temperature to 350°F (180°C), remove the foil and dried beans, and continue to bake the shell until it is golden, about 5 minutes longer. Remove the shell from the oven, cool it briefly, and remove it from the pan. Cool the tart shell completely on a wire rack.

In a small saucepan, heat the jelly with 2 teaspoons water. When the jelly is completely melted, let it cool slightly and then brush half of it carefully over the inside of the tart shell. Let cool.

Arrange the strawberries, pointed-end up, in the tart shell. Glaze the strawberries with the remaining jelly, reheating it if necessary. Let the glaze cool completely before serving.

makes 1 9-inch (23 cm) tart

■ Walnut Wedges

2 cups (280 grams) flour (plain flour)
⅔ cup (150 grams) ground walnuts
1 cup (225 grams) softened sweet butter
½ cup (120 grams) confectioners' sugar
   (icing sugar)
confectioners' sugar (icing sugar)

Combine the flour and ground walnuts in a small bowl. Mix well.

In the large bowl of an electric mixer, cream the butter with the sugar until it is light and fluffy. Add the flour mixture, a little at a time, and mix until a firm dough forms. Cover the bowl with plastic wrap and refrigerate for 30 minutes.

Preheat the oven to 350°F (180°C). Generously butter 2 or more baking or cookie sheets.

Divide the dough into 10 equal pieces. Briefly knead 1 piece at a time until it is slightly softened. Roll the piece into a ball. Put the ball onto a prepared baking sheet and flatten it into a 4-inch (10 cm) round. With the back of a fork, press down the edges of the round. Prick the surface of the cookie all over with the fork. Score the round into quarters, but do not separate it. Repeat the above steps with the remaining dough.

Bake the rounds until well browned, about 20 minutes. Remove the cookies from the oven and cut them into wedges along the scored lines. Using a wide spatula, transfer the wedges to a wire rack. Sift confectioners' sugar (icing sugar) over the cookies. Cool the cookies completely on the rack. Store in an airtight container.

makes 40 cookies

■ Triple Chocolate Cookies

3 ounces (85 grams) semisweet chocolate
1 ounce (30 grams) unsweetened chocolate
1 tablespoon (15 grams) sweet butter
1 egg
⅓ cup (75 grams) packed dark brown sugar
1 tablespoon water
1 teaspoon pure vanilla extract
2 tablespoons (30 grams) sifted flour (plain
   flour)
⅛ teaspoon baking powder
6 ounces (180 grams) semisweet chocolate
   bits
1 cup (225 grams) coarsely chopped walnuts

Melt the semisweet and unsweetened chocolate together in the top of double boiler over hot but not boiling water. Pour the melted chocolate into a mixing bowl and let cool slightly.

Add the egg, brown sugar, water, and vanilla extract to the chocolate mixture. Mix until well blended. Add the flour and baking powder. Stir well. Add the chocolate bits and walnuts and stir until evenly distributed. Cover the bowl with plastic wrap and refrigerate until the dough is firm and easy to handle, about 1 hour.

Preheat the oven to 350°F (180°C). Line two cookie sheets with aluminum foil.

Shape the dough into 1-inch (2.5 cm) balls and put them 1 inch (2.5 cm) apart on the cookie sheets. Bake the cookies until they are slightly firm to the touch, about 13 to 15 mintues.

Remove the cookies from the oven. Slide the foil from the cookie sheets and let the cookies cool completely on the sheets before removing. Store the cookies in an airtight container.

makes 24 to 30 cookies

■ Almond Lemon Cake

½ cup (120 grams) chopped almonds
1⅔ cups (375 grams) sifted, finely ground
*   almonds*
1⅔ cup (375 grams) sifted confectioners'
*   sugar (icing sugar)*
1 egg white
3 very large eggs
2 teaspoons orange-flavored liqueur
2 teaspoons finely grated lemon rind
6 tablespoons (90 grams) cornstarch, sifted
*   together with ½ teaspoon baking powder*
6½ tablespoons (100 grams) sweet butter,
*   melted and cooled*
confectioners' sugar (icing sugar)

Preheat the oven to 350°F (180°C). Generously butter a 9-inch (23 cm) round layer cake pan. Line the bottom of the pan with a piece of waxed paper cut to size. Butter the top of the paper and sprinkle it with flour. Rotate the pan the distribute the flour evenly over the sides. Shake out any excess flour. Press the chopped almonds around the sides of the pan; remove any pieces that fall to the bottom. Set the pan aside.

In the container of a food processor or blender combine the almond meal and sugar. Process until a very fine powder is formed. With the motor running, add the egg white and process until a smooth paste is formed. The paste should feel sticky to the touch.

Put the almond mixture into the large bowl of an electric mixer. Add the eggs, one at a time, beating well after each addition. Continue to beat until the mixture is very light and smooth, about 10 minutes.

Add the orange-flavored liqueur and the lemon rind. Beat for 1 minute longer.

Sift the cornstarch mixture over the bowl and gently fold it into the mixture with a rubber spatula. Shake the batter off the spatula often to avoid lumps. Gently fold in the melted butter.

Turn the batter into the prepared pan. Bake for 40 to 45 minutes, or until a cake tester inserted into the center of the cake comes out clean.

Remove the cake from the oven and cool completely in the pan on a wire rack. Cover the top of the pan with a serving plate. Carefully invert the pan and unmold the cake. Dust the top of the cake with confectioners' sugar (icing sugar) and serve.

makes 1 9-inch (23 cm) cake

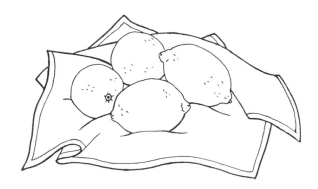

Sauces and Accompaniments

Food should look like food. This may seem obvious but, in fact, too much of what is placed upon the table is masked with garnishes and heavy sauces. The new cuisine has tried to rid the plate of the extraneous. Instead of twelve vegetables and two sauces, an artfully carved bundle of crisp courgettes and the meat or fish placed on top of the sauce can reveal what dinner is all about for the first time.

Sauces should usually not be thickened with flour and eggs. Lighter sauces should reveal more about the principal ingredient, rather than masking it. This, of course, means that those main foods must be of absolutely the best qualilty and cooked to perfection. You cannot disguise the inferior and still hope for applause.

In addition, many possibilities of accompaniments arise: homemade chutneys, purées, flavored butters and mayonnaises, pickled and preserved fruits and nuts—all combine for visual and taste excitement.

But like everything else, use them with discretion and moderation. Too much of a good thing makes for confusion of the palate and the eye and distracts from the main event. Also, arrange the garnishes and sauces with a restrained hand. They should add to, not dominate, the major foods on the plate. Remember the dictum quoted in the introduction: *Faites simple!*

■ Salmon Dill Butter

8 tablespoons (120 grams) softened sweet
    butter
3 ounces (85 grams) smoked salmon, finely
    chopped
1 teaspoon finely chopped fresh dill
1 teaspoon fresh lemon juice
½ teaspoon fresh onion juice

Cream the butter in a mixing bowl until it
is light and fluffy. Add the salmon, dill,
lemon juice and onion juice. Stir with a
wooden spoon until well mixed.

Put the mixture onto a large piece of
plastic wrap. With the help of the plastic
wrap, form the butter into a thick cylinder. To serve, unwrap the butter and slice
it into pats.

makes ¾ cup (180 grams)

■ Green Peppercorn Butter

8 tablespoons (120 grams) softened sweet
    butter
¼ cup (60 grams) finely chopped fresh
    parsley
1 tablespoon green peppercorns, drained
1 teaspoon fresh lemon juice
½ teaspoon Dijon mustard
½ teaspoon Worcestershire sauce
salt to taste, if desired

Combine the butter, parsley, green peppercorns, lemon juice, mustard, Worcestershire sauce and salt in the container of
a blender or food processor. Process until
the mixture is smooth and well combined.

Transfer the mixture to a bowl or crock
and cover. Refrigerate for at least 1½ to 2
hours before using.

makes ½ cup (120 grams)

■ Red Pepper and Shallot Butter Sauce

1½ cups (340 grams) plus 2 tablespoons (30
    grams) sweet butter
2 to 3 medium-sized sweet red peppers,
    seeded and coarsely diced
3 tablespoons finely chopped shallots
2 to 3 tablespoons raspberry vinegar
¼ cup (2 fl oz or 60 ml) fresh lemon juice
½ cup (4 fl oz or 120 ml) dry white wine
¾ teaspoon salt or less if desired

Melt 2 tablespoons (30 grams) of the butter in a saucepan over low heat. When the
foam subsides, add the red peppers and
the shallots. Sauté, stirring constantly,
until the peppers are softened, about 10
minutes.

Add the vinegar to the saucepan and
bring the mixture to a simmer over low
heat. Simmer, uncovered, until the liquid
is reduced by two-thirds, about 5 to 6
minutes.

Add the lemon juice and the wine to the
saucepan. Bring the mixture to a simmer
and cook, uncovered, until the liquid is
reduced by half, about 15 minutes.

Remove the saucepan from the heat
and transfer its contents to the container
of a food processor or blender. Process until the mixture is a smooth purée. Return
the purée to the saucepan.

Cut the remaining butter into 24 equal
pats.

Place the saucepan with the purée over
low heat. Add the butter, one pat at a
time, and whisk until each piece is thoroughly incorporated. Be sure that each
pat is incorporated before adding the
next.

makes 2 cups (16 fl oz or 480 ml)

■ Raspberry Butter Sauce

2 cups (450 grams) fresh raspberries
½ cup (4 fl oz or 120 ml) dry white wine
1½ teaspoons sugar
1 cup (225 grams) sweet butter

Combine the raspberries and the white wine in a saucepan. Bring the mixture to a boil over moderate heat. Cook, uncovered, until the mixture takes on a jamlike consistency, about 15 minutes. Stir frequently. Remove the mixture from the heat and taste. Add the sugar, more or less depending on the tartness of the raspberries.

Transfer the mixture to the container of a food processor or blender. Process until the mixture is a smooth purée. Return the purée to the saucepan.

Cut the butter into 16 equal pats.

Place the saucepan with the purée over low heat. Add the butter, one pat at a time, and whisk until each piece is thoroughly incorporated. Be sure that each pat is incorporated before adding the next.

After all the butter has been added, strain the mixture through a fine sieve set over a small bowl. Press the mixture through the sieve with the back of a spoon. Discard any solids left in the sieve.

Serve at once or keep the sauce warm over hot water for up to 1 hour.

makes 2 cups (16 fl oz or 480 ml)

■ Horseradish Cream

1 cup (8 fl oz or 160 ml) chilled heavy cream (single cream)
2 teaspoons sugar
½ teaspoon salt, if desired
3 tablespoons (45 grams) drained prepared white horseradish

Combine the cream, sugar and salt in a well-chilled bowl. Beat until the cream forms stiff peaks. Fold in the horseradish.

makes 2¼ cups (18 fl oz or 540 ml)

■ Tarragon Marinade

1 cup (8 fl oz or 240 ml) olive oil
⅓ cup (3 fl oz or 80 ml) fresh lemon juice
3 green onions (scallions), thinly sliced (including green parts)
2 teaspoons dried tarragon
2 teaspoons Dijon-style mustard
½ teaspoon salt, if desired
freshly ground black pepper

Combine the olive oil, lemon juice, green onions, tarragon, mustard, salt and black pepper to taste in a bowl. Beat with a wire whisk until well blended.

Makes 1⅓ cups (11 fl oz or 320 ml)

■ White Wine Marinade

3 tablespoons olive oil
1 cup (225 grams) finely chopped onion
3 garlic cloves, finely chopped
¼ cup (2 fl oz or 60 ml) tarragon vinegar
1 cup (8 fl oz or 240 ml) dry white wine
1 teaspoon dried thyme
1 teaspoon crumbled dried rosemary
1 bay leaf
6 parsley sprigs
6 black peppercorns

Heat the olilve oil in a saucepan over moderate heat. Add the onions and garlic and cook, stirring constantly, until the onions are soft, about 5 minutes.

Add the vinegar and raise the heat to moderately high. Cook until the mixture is reduced by half.

Add the wine, thyme, rosemary, bay leaf, parsley and peppercorns. Bring the mixture to a boil, then reduce the heat and simmer for 5 minutes.

Remove the saucepan from the heat and let the marinade cool. When the marinade is cool, pour it into a shallow bowl or dish and marinate the food.

makes 1½ cups (12 fl oz or 360 ml)

■ Mustard Vodka Sauce

1½ cups (12 fl oz or 360 ml) chicken broth
2 tablespoons finely chopped onions
½ teaspoon finely chopped garlic
1 1-ounce (30 grams) slice stale dark
  pumpernickel bread, coarsely torn
½ teaspoon caraway seeds
freshly ground black pepper
1¼ tablespoons grainy mustard
1½ teaspoons Dijon-style mustard
1½ tablespoons vodka
1 tablespoon finely chopped chives or green
  onions (scallions)

Combine the chicken broth, onions, and garlic in a saucepan. Cover the saucepan and bring to a simmer over high heat. Reduce the heat and simmer until the onions are completely cooked, about 10 minutes. Add the bread and cook until it is soaked through, about 35 seconds longer.

Transfer the mixture to the container of a food processor or blender. Process until the mixture is very smooth. Return the mixture to the saucepan. Add the caraway seeds and black pepper to taste.

Cook over moderately high heat until the sauce is thick and reduced to a little more than 1 cup (8 fl oz or 240 ml), about 6 minutes. Add both mustards, the vodka and the chives. Stir until well blended and serve.

makes 1 cup (8 fl oz or 240 ml)

■ Aromatic Olive Oil

1 cup (8 fl oz or 240 ml) extra-virgin olive oil
1½ tablespoons sliced fresh basil leaves
1 tablespoon finely chopped fresh parsley
2 anchovy fillets, rinsed, drained, and very
  finely chopped
½ teaspoon grated lemon rind
¼ teaspoon very finely chopped garlic
¼ teaspoon coarse salt
⅛ teaspoon freshly ground black pepper

Combine the olive oil, basil, parsley, anchovies, lemon rind, garlic, salt and pepper in a 2-cup (16 fl oz or 480 ml) jar with a tightly fitting lid. Close the jar tightly and shake well.

Let the jar stand at room temperature for 2 to 3 hours. Shake jar until ingredients are well mixed before using.

makes 1 cup (8 fl oz or 240 ml)

■ Mango Chutney

3 ripe mangos, peeled and cut into thin
  strips
2 cups (16 fl oz or 480 ml) distilled white
  vinegar
1 cup (225 grams) sugar
1 cup (225 grams) packed dark brown sugar
1 cup (225 grams) finely chopped onion
3 garlic cloves, finely chopped
½ teaspoon freshly ground black pepper
1 teaspoon salt
1 teaspoon chili powder
2 tablespoons finely chopped ginger root
1½ teaspoons cinnamon
¼ teaspoon ground cloves
1 teaspoon ground allspice
1 teaspoon mustard seeds
½ cup (120 grams) dark raisins
½ cup (120 grams) dried currants
1½ pounds (675 grams) sweet apples, peeled,
  cored and coarsely chopped

Combine the mangos, vinegar, sugar, brown sugar, onion, garlic, pepper, salt, chili powder, ginger, cinnamon, cloves, allspice, mustard seeds, raisins, currants and apples in a large mixing bowl. Stir until the mixture is well combined. Cover the bowl and refrigerate overnight.

Transfer the mixture to a very large pot or kettle. Bring the mixture to a boil, then reduce the heat and simmer, stirring often, until the mixture is thick and syrupy, about 30 minutes. Transfer the mixture to hot sterililzed jars. Seal, cool, and store for at least 1 month before using.

makes 5 cups (1.35 kg)

■ Crème Frâiche Method I

1 cup (8 fl oz or 240 ml) heavy cream (single cream)

1 cup (225 grams) sour cream

Do not use ultrapasteurized cream for this recipe.

Combine the heavy cream (single cream) and the sour cream in a small bowl. Whisk to blend well.

Cover the bowl loosely with aluminum foil and let stand in a warm place overnight or until thick. This could take 12 or more hours.

Cover the bowl tightly and refrigerate for at least 12 hours before serving. Crème frâiche will keep in the refrigerator for about 5 to 7 days if it is tightly covered.

makes 2 cups (16 fl oz or 480 ml)

■ Crème Frâiche Method II

1 cup (8 fl oz or 240 ml) heavy cream (single cream)

1 to 2 tablespoons buttermilk

Do not use ultrapasteurized cream for this recipe.

Combine the heavy cream (single cream) and the buttermilk (the more buttermilk is used, the tangier the flavor) in a jar with a tightly fitting lid. Cover the jar tightly and shake it until the ingredients are well combined, about 1 to 2 minutes. Let the jar stand at room temperature overnight or until thick. This could take 10 to 12 hours.

Refrigerate the crème frâiche for at least 12 hours before serving. It will keep in the refrigerator for about 5 to 7 days if it is tightly covered.

makes 1 cup (8 fl oz or 240 ml)

■ Clarified Butter

1 cup (225 grams) sweet butter, cut into small pieces

Melt the butter in a small saucepan over low heat. Remove the saucepan from the heat and let the white milk solids settle to the bottom. Skim the foam from the top of the butter with a spoon.

Line a fine mesh sieve with a double layer of cheesecloth. Strain the yellow liquid in the saucepan through the sieve into a container with a tightly fitting lid. Discard any solids that remain in the sieve. Cover the container tightly and refrigerate until needed. Clarified butter will keep almost indefinitely if kept tightly covered and well chilled.

makes ¾ cup (6 fl oz or 180 ml)

Index